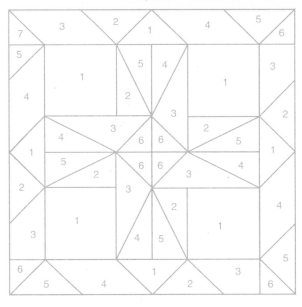

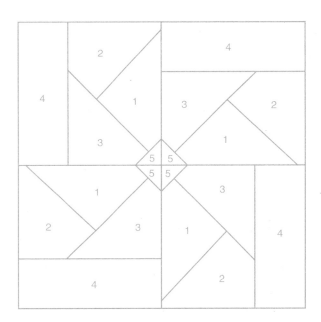

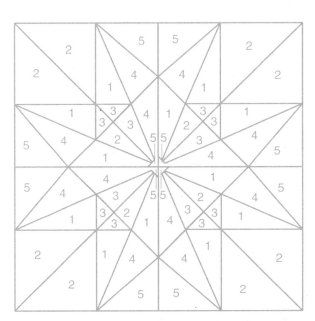

Beautiful Foundation–Pieced Quilt Blocks

by Mary Jo Hiney

Sterling Publishing Co., Inc. New York

A Sterling/Chapelle Book

For Chapelle Limited
Owner: Jo Packham
Editor: Ann Bear

Staff: Marie Barber, Areta Bingham, Kass Burchett, Rebecca Christensen, Holly Fuller, Marilyn Goff, Shirley Heslop, Holly Hollingsworth, Sherry Hoppe, Shawn Hsu, Susan Jorgensen, Pauline Locke, Barbara Milburn, Linda Orton, Karmen Quinney, Leslie Ridenour, Cindy Stoeckl

Photography: Kevin Dilley, Photographer for Hazen Photography

We would like to offer our sincere appreciation of the valuable support given in this ever-changing industry of new ideas, concepts, designs, and products. Several projects shown in this publication were created with the outstanding and innovative products developed by:

Benartex, Inc.
1460 Bradway
New York, NY 10036
(212) 840-3250

Fiskars Scissors
P.O. Box 8027
Wausau, WI 54402-2091
(715) 842-2091

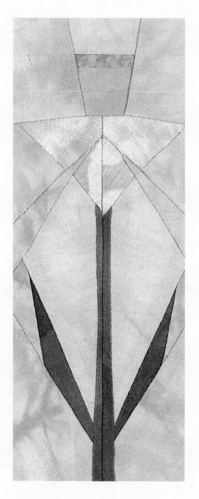

Library of Congress Cataloging-in-Publication Data

Hiney, Mary Jo.
    Beautiful foundation-pieced quilt blocks / by Mary Jo Hiney.'
        p.   cm.
    "A Sterling/Chapele book."
    Includes index.
    ISBN 0-8069-3797-1
    1. Patchwork--Patterns.   2. Machine quilting.
    3. Patchwork quilts. I. Title.
    TT835.H458 1999   98-46007
    746.46'041--dc21   CIP

10   9   8   7   6   5   4   3   2   1

Published by Sterling Publishing Company, Inc.
387 Park Avenue South, New York, N.Y. 10016
© 1999 by Chapelle Limited
Distributed in Canada by Sterling Publishing
c/o Canadian Manda Group, One Atlantic Avenue, Suite 105
Toronto, Ontario, Canada M6K 3E7
Distributed in Great Britain and Europe by Cassell PLC
Wellington House, 125 Strand, London WC2R 0BB, England
Distributed in Australia by Capricorn Link (Australia) Pty Ltd.
P.O. Box 6651, Baulkham Hills, Business Centre, NSW 2153,
Australia
Printed in United States of America

Sterling ISBN 0-8069-3797-1

If you have any questions or comments, please contact:
Chapelle, Ltd., Inc.
P.O. Box 9252
Ogden, UT 84409
(801) 621-2777
(801) 621-2788 Fax
chapelle1@aol.com

Table of Contents

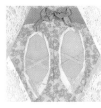

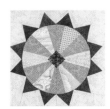

Beautiful Foundation–Pieced Quilt Blocks is designed with the beginning quilter in mind. The technique of foundation piecing is a quick and easy way to make beautiful, complex–looking quilt blocks without the time associated with traditional piecing.

Foundation piecing is sewing fabric pieces to a foundation, such as paper or fabric, following a numerical sequence. Lines are drawn on the wrong side of the foundation. Fabric is placed on the unmarked (right) side of the foundation with right side up and sewn on the marked (wrong) side. This technique allows the quilter to piece even the smallest pieces more quickly and accurately, since all sewing follows drawn lines.

Provided with each quilt block in this book are a full–color photograph of the actual block, its size, level of difficulty, full–sized pattern pieces for tracing onto your foundation, a full–color unit placement diagram of the assembled block, and a black and white seam line diagram of the assembled block. Many of these blocks are made of separate units. The colored diagram indicates how each unit is placed in the block. The black and white diagram indicates seams.

When reading the seam line diagram, blue lines indicate a seam and magenta dots indicate where units must be matched together. When there are two or more of one unit in a block, only one seam is indicated with blue lines.

MATERIALS & TOOLS

Size and quantity of materials will depend on project and size desired. If planning a quilt, please refer to Planning a Quilt on page 9 for dimensions.

Materials

Batting

Binding: bias, quilt

Fabrics: colors of choice, cotton, for backing, foundation, and binding; colors of choice, cotton scraps, for foundation piecing

Interfacing: lightweight, nonwoven, or tear–away, for foundation

Thread: coordinating color, cotton

Tools

Fabric glue stick

Iron and ironing board

Needles: quilting; sewing

Paper: computer, copy, newsprint, notebook, or tracing, for foundation; tracing

Pen or pencil: for marking and transferring

Pins: quilt; safety

Quilting frame

Rotary cutter and cutting board

Ruler: Quilter's, small and large

Scissors: craft; fabric

Sewing machine

Spray bottle

FABRIC

Cotton fabric is recommended for all projects in this book. Pieces will stay in place easily after finger–pressing. Some quilt–blocks shown in this book are made with silks and velvets for added beauty. Keep in mind these fabrics are more difficult to work with. Finger–pressing will not stay in place with these fabrics or others, such as polyester cotton. They will need to be pinned, glued, or iron–pressed in place after each step. If planning a quilt, please refer to Planning a Quilt on page 9 for dimensions.

If planning to make a washable project, test fabric to make certain it is colorfast and preshrunk. Do not trust labels. For the puckered look of an antique quilt, use fabrics with various shrinkage differences and do not preshrink.

If this is not the desired look, wash and dry all fabrics before beginning. Fabrics that continue to shrink, after washing and drying several times, should not be used for quilt block projects.

To test for color fastness and shrinkage:

1. Cut a 2"-wide strip of each fabric, using fabric scissors.

2. Place each fabric strip separately into a clean bowl of extremely hot water, or hold each fabric strip under hot running water. If unsure fabric is colorfast, place wet strip on a dry paper towel, and watch for bleeding on the paper towel.

3. If fabric strip bleeds a great deal, wash all of that fabric until excess dye washes out. Fabrics that continue to bleed, after washing several times, should not be used for quilt block projects.

4. To test for shrinkage, iron each saturated strip dry, using a hot iron.

5. When fabric strip is completely dry, measure and compare it to original measurements.

Cutting the Fabric

For foundation piecing, pieces do not have to be cut perfectly. Use strips, rectangles, squares, or any odd-shaped scrap material. Make certain fabric is at least ⅜" larger on all sides than the area it is to cover. As triangle shapes are more difficult to piece, use generous-sized fabric pieces and position pieces carefully on the foundation. Some fabric is wasted using foundation piecing, but the time saved is well worth it.

FOUNDATION MATERIAL

Decide what type of foundation to use for piecing the blocks — lightweight interfacing, fabric, paper, or tear-away interfacing. For fabric, choose a light-colored, lightweight fabric that can be seen through for tracing. Batiste, muslin, and broadcloth work well and will give extra stability to the blocks. For paper, choose one that can be seen through, such as tracing paper, copy paper, newsprint, or computer paper. For greatest speed and least bulk, use the lightest-weight nonwoven interfacing for foundation. Use a light touch when preparing the foundation.

Note: Keep in mind that using a fabric foundation will add another layer to quilt through. Paper tears away after sewing is completed. For tear-away interfacing, choose a type that can be removed easily.

MIRROR IMAGE

Foundation quilting will create a mirror image of the pattern. If an exact replica of the pattern is desired, reverse the pattern on the foundation, following the method for mirrored image units below. The patterns shown are a mirror image of the photograph shown. This book has been designed so each set of patterns and instructions will result in an exact image of the photograph shown.

Many of the quilt blocks in *Beautiful Foundation-Pieced Quilt Blocks* have left and right mirrored units. Only one pattern is given. Trace two unit patterns, but make one unit pattern on the wrongside. This is just one advantage to using a see-through foundation. If a see-through foundation is not used, make a copy of the pattern. Flip the paper over and hold up to a light source and trace onto foundation.

Note: Mirrored units are represented on colored unit placement diagrams with (m). For example: A(m).

PREPARING THE FOUNDATION

Tracing the Block

1. Trace pattern onto foundation material, using a ruler and a fine–point permanent marker or a #2 pencil. Include all numbers.

2. Draw ¼" seam allowance around outside edges.

3. Cut foundation ½" from seam allowance of the block or unit.

4. Repeat for number of blocks needed for project.

Tip: If desiring a block to look exactly like the pattern, reverse pattern before tracing onto paper, then trace onto foundation material.

Transferring the Block

Another method of pattern transfer is to transfer pattern onto foundation material, using a transfer tool. Include all numbers.

STEP BY STEP INSTRUCTIONS FOR FOUNDATION PIECING

Note: Instructional photos show assembly of Flower Bouquet quilt block found on page 34.

1. Transfer pattern onto foundation, as shown in Photo 1, using a #2 pencil or a fine–point permanent marking pen; write all numbers on foundation. Mark for a mirror image, if applicable.

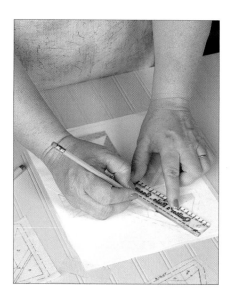

Photo 1:

Use a #2 pencil or a fine–point permanent marking pen to transfer pattern to foundation.

Photo 2:

Place fabric piece 2 on fabric piece 1, right sides together. Pin, glue, or hold in place.

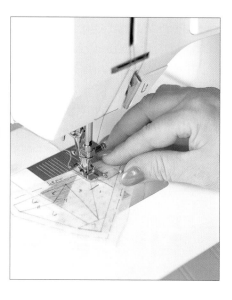

Photo 3:

Stitch fabric piece 2 to fabric piece 1 along line between shapes 1 and 2. Repeat with unit A(m), stitching on unmarked side of foundation. Begin and end two or three stitches beyond line.

2. Cut fabric pieces for block. Make a chart as an aid to note fabrics, number placements, cut sizes, and quantities needed for each fabric.

3. Turn over foundation with unmarked side up. Place fabric piece 1, right side up, on shape 1. If foundation is not sheer, hold foundation up to a light source to make certain that fabric overlaps at least ¼" on all sides of shape 1. Pin, glue, or hold in place.

4. Make certain that fabric piece 2 overlaps at least ¼" on all sides of shape 2. Place fabric piece 2 on fabric piece 1, right sides together, as shown in Photo 2 on page 6. Duplicate steps for mirror image unit A(m) while making unit A. Be certain fabric is placed on correct side to make mirror image.

5. Turn over foundation, with marked side up. Sew along line between shapes 1 and 2, with marked side of foundation up, using a very small stitch (this is helpful if paper has been used as the foundation). Begin and end two or three stitches beyond line, as shown in Photo 3 on page 6. Trim excess fabric ⅛" to ¼" past seam line.

6. Turn over foundation, with unmarked side up. Open fabric piece 2 and finger–press seam. Pin or glue in place, if necessary.

7. Make certain that fabric piece 3 overlaps at least ¼" on all sides of shape 3. Place fabric piece 3 on fabric piece 1, with right sides together. Pin, glue, or hold in place.

8. Turn over foundation, with marked side up. Sew along line between shapes 1 and 3. Begin and end sewing two or three stitches beyond line. Trim excess fabric ⅛" to ¼" from seam line, being careful to not cut into foundation material when trimming, as shown in Photo 4.

9. Turn over foundation, with unmarked side up. Open fabric piece 3, finger–press seam. Pin or glue in place, if necessary. Continue sewing and trimming fabric pieces in numerical order through piece 5.

Photo 4:

Trim excess fabric ⅛" to ¼" from seam line. Fabric may be trimmed prior to stitching.

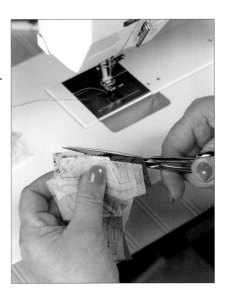

Photo 5:

To preseam, first trim the seam area. Next, trim the pieces to shape that must be preseamed.

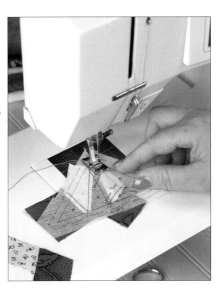

Photo 6:

Third, seam the trimmed pieces. Last, stitch preseamed piece in place on foundation.

10. Some blocks require **preseamed pieces**. This is designated by a mark (**"**) on the patterns at the seam. To preseam, first trim fabric pieces 4–5 that are already on the foundation ¼" past seam line. With marked side of foundation face up, place foundation piece 6, wrong side up, on shape 6, extending piece ¼" over 4–5 seam line. Trim piece at preseam ¼" past seam line. Set piece 6 aside. Place fabric piece 6a, wrong side up, on shape 6a and trim at the preseam in the same manner, as shown in Photo 5 on page 7. Stitch trimmed pieces together, taking a ¼" seam and press seam open. Stitch fabric piece 6–6a to fabric pieces 4–5, right sides together, matching preseam to seam between 4–5, as shown in Photo 6 on page 7. It will be necessary to pin the preseamed piece in place where the seams must match. Before stitching, fold pinned piece open, checking placement. Alter seam line of 6–6a if necessary.

11. Press the unit when all fabric pieces are stitched to foundation. Stitch in between seam allowance around all edges. Use a ruler to trim unit even at the ¼" seam allowance markings, as shown in Photo 7.

12. Pin unit A to unit A(m), right sides together, matching at dots. Stitch, taking a ¼" seam. Press seam open. Blocks having angled seams may need to be clipped prior to stitching. Clip unit B to inner seam where it angles upward. Pin and stitch unit B to assembled unit A–A(m), right sides together, with a ¼" seam, as shown in Photo 8. Press seam open.

Photo 7:

After stitching in between the seam allowance, trim away excess fabric, using a rotary cutter.

Photo 8:

Stitch units together, matching at dots for assembly, following individual block instructions. Clip angled seams, if necessary.

BACKING & BATTING

Backing

Use cotton fabric for quilt backing. If hand–sewing quilt, avoid bed sheets for backing. They are difficult to quilt through. When making a bed–sized quilt, the fabric may need to be pieced to fit the quilt top.

Batting

Batting is traditionally used as the middle layer of a quilt or sometimes in clothing and doll making. There are numerous types of batting available. Bonded cotton batting gives a flat, natural appearance and will require a great deal of quilting to secure layers, with quilting lines less than 1" apart. Felt may be substituted and renders the same appearance as bonded cotton. Polyester batting gives a puffy appearance and is a good choice for machine quilting. Thick batting is recommended for tied quilts.

Tip: Remove batting from the package a day before using. Open it out to full size. This will help the batting lay flat.

QUILT ASSEMBLY

Planning a Quilt

Determine the quilt size desired, using the following guidelines:

Bed Type	Mattress Measurements
Crib	27" x 51"
Twin	39" x 75"
Double	54" x 75"
Queen	60" x 80"
King	76" x 80"

A small wall quilt can be any size, and easily completed in a short time.

Add the drop (part of the quilt hanging over edge of the mattress) and tuck (part tucking under the pillows) to the mattress measurements.

Example: If desiring the quilt to hang 12" over the edge of the mattress with a 12" tuck, add 24" to the length and width of the mattress size.

Example: For a twin–sized quilt, made with 7" x 7" blocks and a finished size of 63" x 99", use 60 blocks. Sew six blocks across and ten rows down, with 2" sashing in between blocks and rows, and around outer edge. Finish quilt with a 3½" border.

Sizing Quilt Blocks

1. Lay out the quilt blocks in design order on your work surface. Measure each block vertically and horizontally and chart the measurements. Once sewn, the individual quilt blocks will not be square. Some edges will shrink and some will grow. Use your chart to find the smallest block measurement that must be used as the basis for trimming each block. Be certain to determine which block edge measurements must be identical.

Example: For the Teasing Kitty quilt assembly on page 14, Kitty Cat blocks must be square. Vertical measurement of each Kitty Cat and Flower Spray block must be the same. The horizontal measurement of each Mousy block must be the same as vertical measurement of Kitty Cat and Flower Spray blocks.

2. Trim quilt blocks so they are trued up (square) and equally sized in relationship to each other, using a quilter's ruler, rotary cutter, and cutting board with grid lines. Leave a ¼" seam allowance around all edges.

Sashing & Borders

Sashing is done by sewing fabric around quilt blocks, in order to set them apart from each other. Sashing can be sewn either to vertical or horizontal edges first. An inner border sets the assembled quilt apart from the outer border or binding.

1. Measure vertical or horizontal edges of quilt block. Cut sashing according to quantity and width desired. By cutting sashing identical in size, it will be easy to keep the quilt square.

2. Sew blocks and sashing together in rows. Press seams.

3. Sew rows of blocks and sashing together.

4. Measure the vertical or horizontal edges of an assembled quilt top. Cut outer sashing or border strips to quantity and width desired.

5. Sew outer sashing or border strips to long sides of quilt. Press seams toward border.

6. If additional borders are needed, repeat Steps 4 and 5.

7. Remove foundation from squares, if applicable.

Tip: For easier paper removal, dampen foundation paper, using a spray bottle of water.

Quilt Layers

Layer quilt with backing, batting, and quilt top.

1. Place fabric for quilt back onto work surface, wrong side up. Stretch and secure fabric to work surface, using masking tape or pins.

2. Layer batting, right side up, over quilt back fabric.

3. Center and place wrong side of quilt top over batting. Pin–baste the three layers together. If planning to hand–quilt, thread–baste the three layers together.

4. Remove masking tape from backing fabric edges. Hand–quilt at this time, if desired.

Quilt Binding

Binding finishes the edges of the quilt. It can also be the outer border.

1. Measure top and bottom edges of quilt for binding. If measurements are different, cut fabric for binding to an in–between length. Sew binding to quilt top and bottom edges through all layers, stretching either binding strip or quilt edge for a perfect fit.

2. Trim batting and quilt back flush with quilt top. Press seams toward binding.

3. Fold binding around to back, with folded edge flush to batting edge. Turn raw edge of binding under ¼", or as necessary, to enclose seam. Pin binding in place.

4. Measure quilt sides and add 1½" to measurement. Cut and sew binding to sides, extending fabric strip ¾" beyond top and bottom quilt edges. Trim batting and quilt back flush with quilt top.

5. Press seams toward binding. At corners, turn extended binding fabric inward, then fold binding around to back and proceed, using the same technique as used for top and bottom quilt edges. Make certain to keep corners square. Use a blind stitch to hand–sew binding in place.

Marking the Quilting Design

Before marking on the quilt top, test marking material on fabric to make certain it will wash out.

Mark all quilting lines on right side of fabric, using a marking tool. Marked lines will not show if quilting is done over the top of lines.

Note: Marking lines may become permanent when using a hot iron on fabric.

Avoid marking quilting lines if quilter can gauge accurately while sewing around shapes. Marking is not necessary for a tied quilt or when quilting in the ditch of a seam. Other quilting techniques may require marking.

Quilting the Quilt

The quilt can be machine or hand sewn.

Note: Hand quilting may be more difficult if fabric was used as a foundation since there is an extra layer of fabric to quilt through.

If the quilter has never used a sewing machine for quilting, refer to a more tutorial book for this technique. A quilter can quiltg a quilt, using almost any home sewing machine. Make certain the machine is oiled and in good working condition. An even–feed foot is recommended, since it is designed to feed the top and bottom layers of the quilt through the machine evenly.

To quilt in the ditch of the seam, pull blocks or pieces apart, and machine stitch tightly in between the two pieces. Keep stitching to side of seam, to avoid bulky seam allowance under it. The machine sewn quilt lines will be hidden in the seam.

Free–form machine quilting is done on a sewing machine, using a darning foot, with the feed dogs down. It can be used to quilt around a design or a motif. Free–form machine quilting takes practice. The quilter controls the quilt through the machine rather than the machine moving the quilt. This technique allows quilting in any direction without pivoting the quilt around the needle.

Project Ideas

Tote Bag

Made with quilt squares found in Chapter 7 on pages 60–68.

Vest

Made with quilt squares found in Chapter 10 on pages 94–105.

Fabric–covered Box

Made with quilt squares found in Chapter 1 on pages 16–23.

Mini Quilt

Made with quilt squares found in Chapter 2 on pages 24–31.

Pillow

Made with quilt squares found in Chapter 3 on pages 32–41.

Just one example of many quilt possibilities.

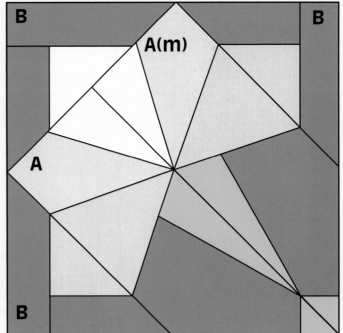

Unit Placement Diagram

NOSEGAY
4" block (moderate)

Note: This block may be made as an 8" block by joining four blocks.

1. Make one unit A. Make one mirror image of unit A. Make three of unit B.

2. Sew unit A to mirror image unit A(m), matching at dots for assembly.

3. Sew one unit B to top and each side of unit A–A(m), matching at dots for assembly.

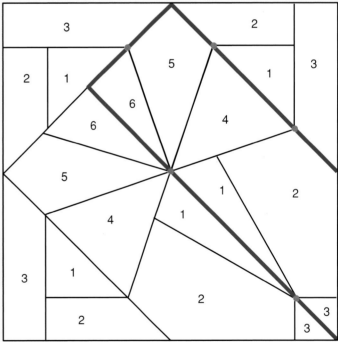

Seam Line Diagram

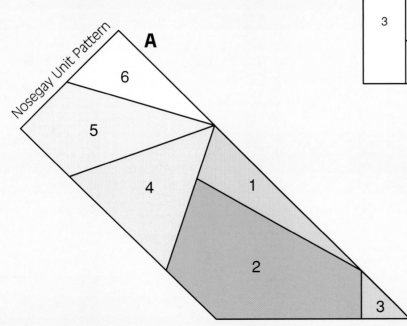

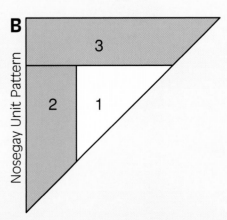

FROG KING
6" block (moderate)

1. Make one each of units A, B, and C. Make one mirror image each of units A, B, and C.

2. Sew units A, B, and C together in alphabetical order, matching at dots for assembly. Repeat for mirror image units A(m), B(m), C(m).

3. Sew unit A–B–C to mirror image unit A(m)–B(m)–C(m), matching at dots for assembly.

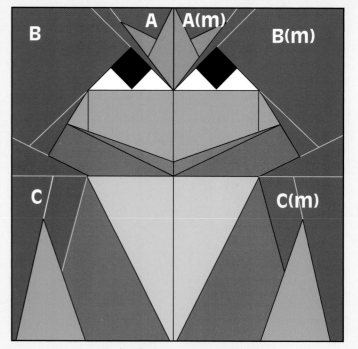

Unit Placement Diagram

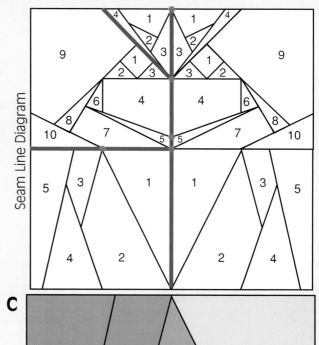

Seam Line Diagram

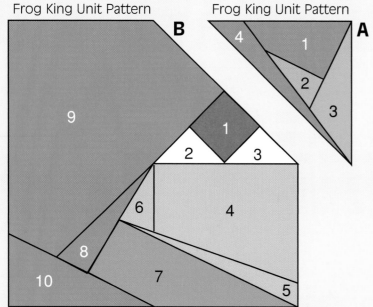

Frog King Unit Pattern

Frog King Unit Pattern

Frog King Unit Pattern

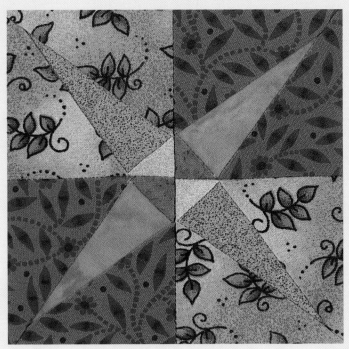

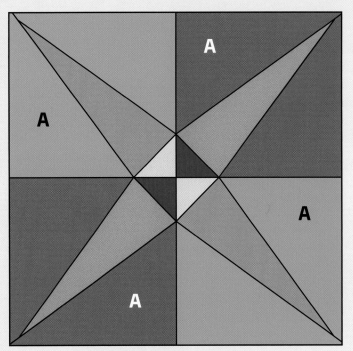

Unit Placement Diagram

DIAGONAL CANOES
4" block (easy)

Note: This block may be made as an 8" block by joining four blocks.

1. Make four of unit A, alternating colors as shown.

2. Sew four units A together, matching at dots for assembly.

Diagonal Canoes Unit Pattern

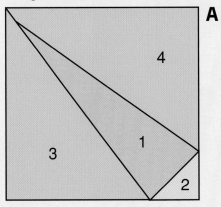

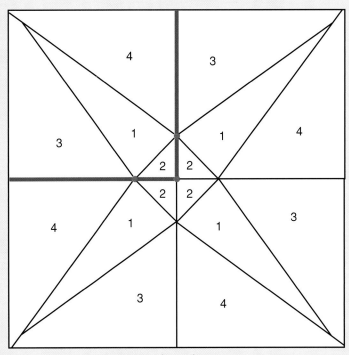

Seam Line Diagram

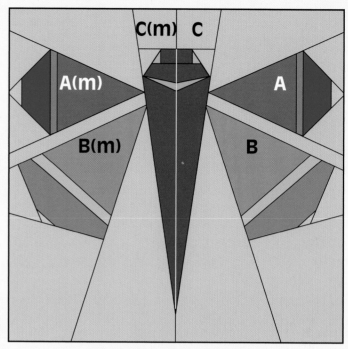

Unit Placement Diagram

DRAGONFLY
6" block (moderate)

1. Make one each of units A, B, and C. Make one mirror image each of units A, B, and C.

2. Sew units A, B, and C together in alphabetical order, matching at dots for assembly. Repeat for mirror image units A(m), B(m), C(m).

3. Sew unit A–B–C to mirror image unit A(m)–B(m)–C(m), matching at dots for assembly.

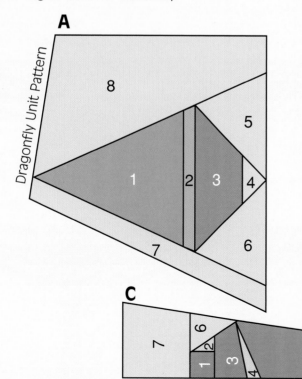

Seam Line Diagram

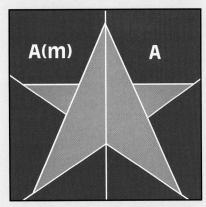

Unit Placement Diagram

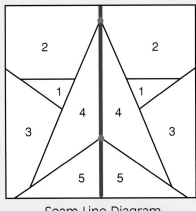

Seam Line Diagram

SMALL STAR
2" block (easy)

1. Make one unit A. Make one mirror image of unit A.

2. Sew unit A to mirror image unit A(m), matching at dots for assembly.

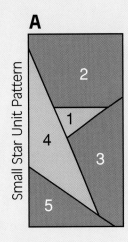

A

Small Star Unit Pattern

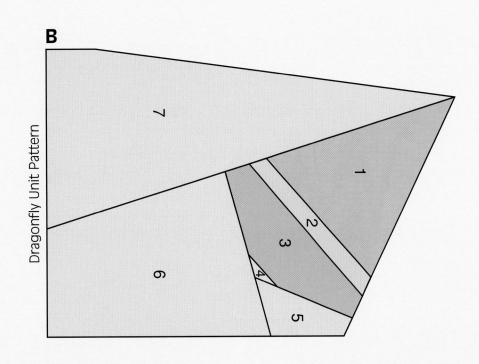

B

Dragonfly Unit Pattern

WESTERN STAR
8" block (moderate)

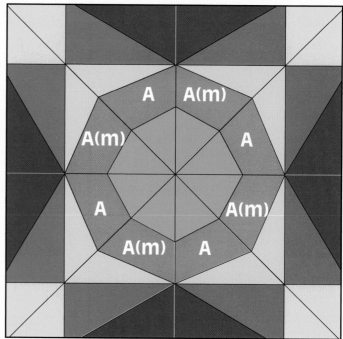

Unit Placement Diagram

Note: This block may be made as a 4" block by reducing pattern 50%.

1. Make four of unit A. Make four mirror images of unit A.

2. Sew each unit A to a mirror image unit A(m), matching at dots for assembly.

3. Sew four units A–A(m) together, matching at dots for assembly.

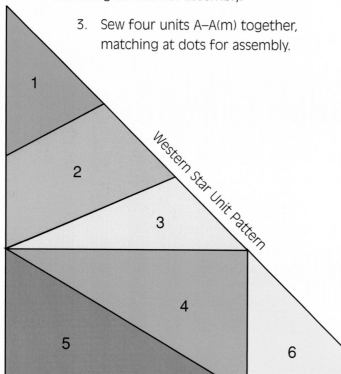

Western Star Unit Pattern

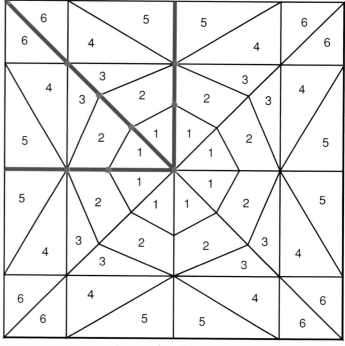

Seam Line Diagram

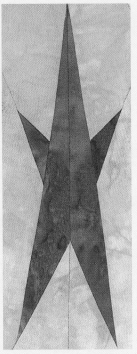

NARROW STAR

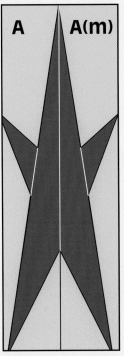

Unit Placement
Diagram

Seam Line
Diagram

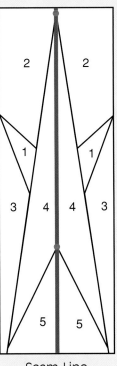

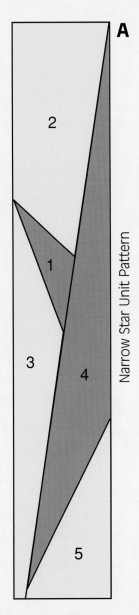

Narrow Star Unit Pattern

NARROW AND WIDE STARS
2" x 6" blocks (easy)

Note: Instructions apply to two separate blocks.

1. Make one unit A. Make one mirror image of unit A.

2. Sew unit A to mirror image unit A(m), matching at dots for assembly.

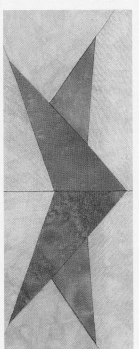

WIDE STAR

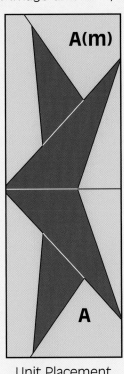

Unit Placement
Diagram

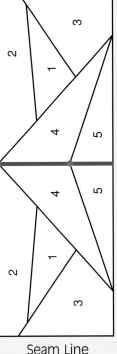

Seam Line
Diagram

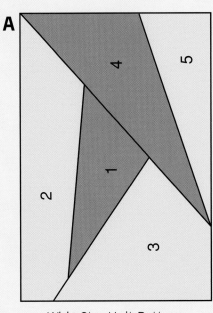

Wide Star Unit Pattern

page 23

Chapter 2

Terracotta Terrace

Just one example of many quilt possibilities.

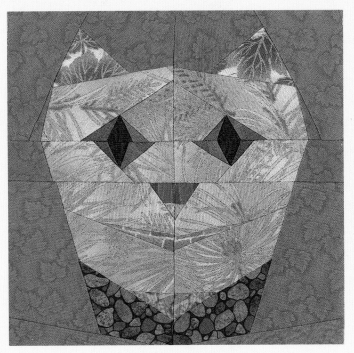

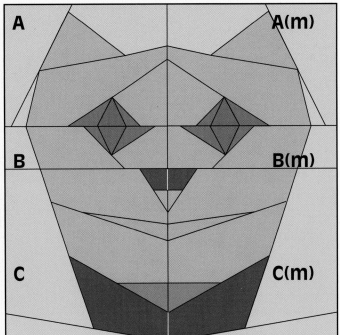

KITTY CAT
6" block (moderate)

Note: Pieces 6 and 6a are preseamed before sewing to unit A and mirror image unit A(m). See preseam instructions on page 8.

1. Make one each of units A, B, and C. Make one mirror image each of units A, B, and C.

2. Sew each unit to its mirror image, matching at dots for assembly.

3. Sew units A–A(m), B–B(m), and C–C(m) together in alphabetical order, matching at dots for assembly.

Unit Placement Diagram

Seam Line Diagram

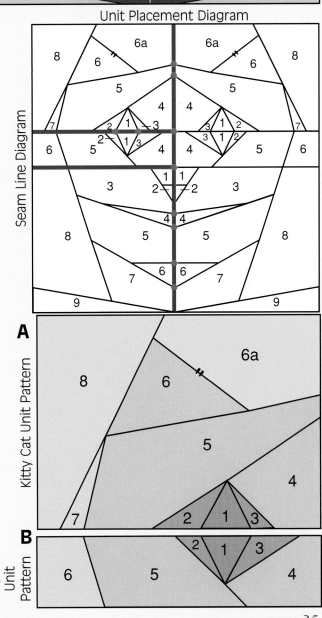

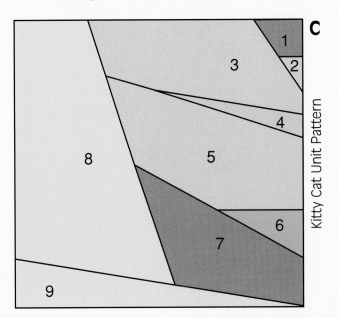

Kitty Cat Unit Pattern

Kitty Cat Unit Pattern

Kitty Cat Unit Pattern

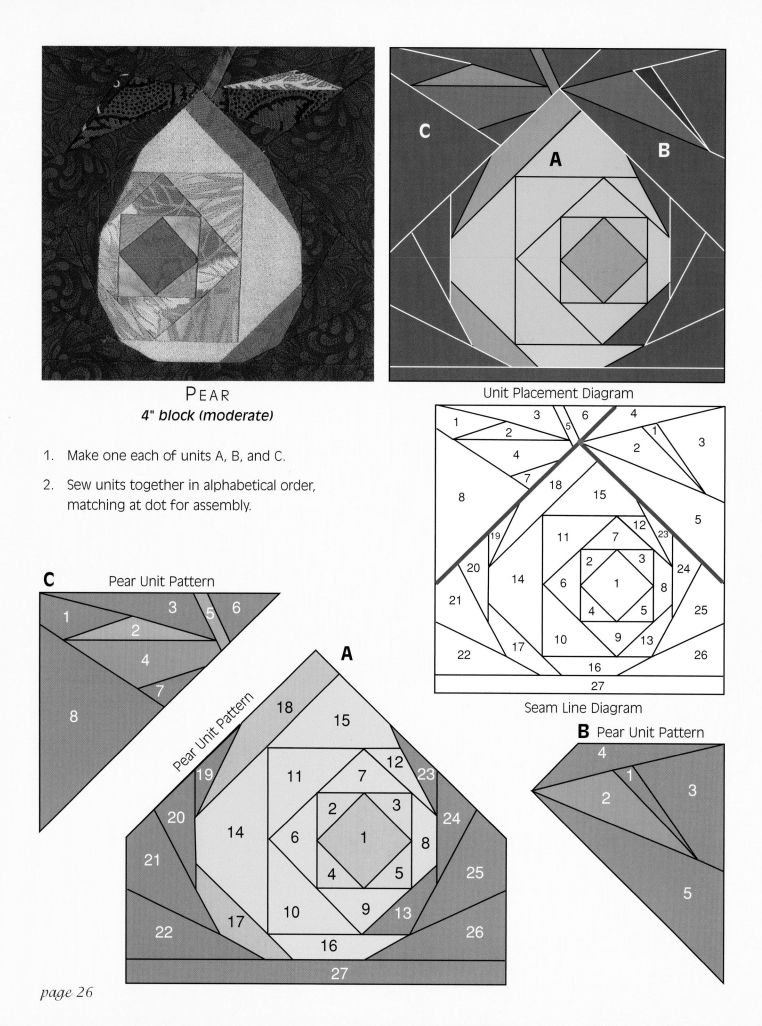

PEAR
4" block (moderate)

1. Make one each of units A, B, and C.

2. Sew units together in alphabetical order, matching at dot for assembly.

Unit Placement Diagram

Seam Line Diagram

C Pear Unit Pattern

A Pear Unit Pattern

B Pear Unit Pattern

CHRYSANTHEMUM
4" block (moderate)

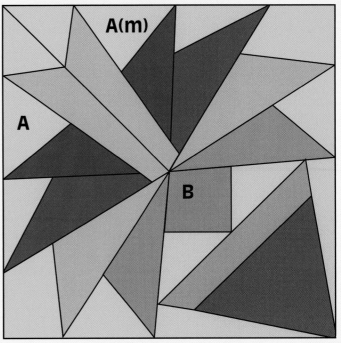

Unit Placement Diagram

Note: This block may be made as an 8" block by joining four blocks.

1. Make one each of units A and B. Make one mirror image of unit A.

2. Sew unit A to mirror image unit A(m), matching at dots for assembly.

3. Clip unit B to seam line at dot. Sew unit B to unit A–A(m), matching at dot for assembly.

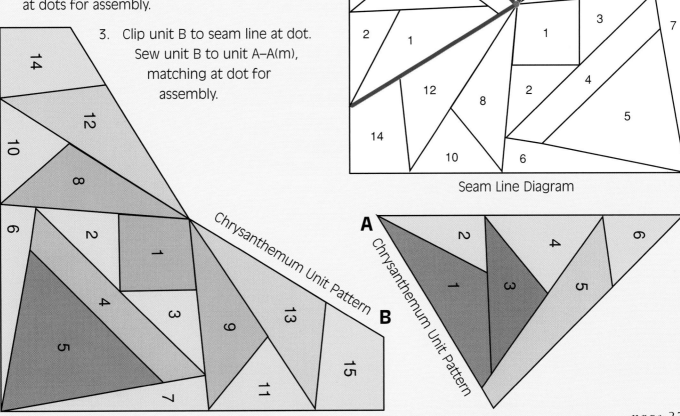

Seam Line Diagram

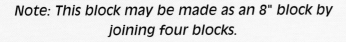

Chrysanthemum Unit Pattern

F L O W E R S P R A Y
2" x 6" block (moderate)

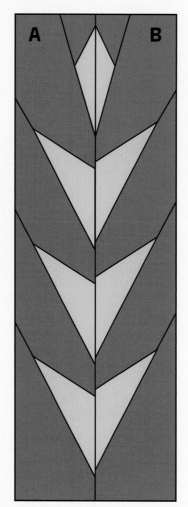

Unit Placement Diagram

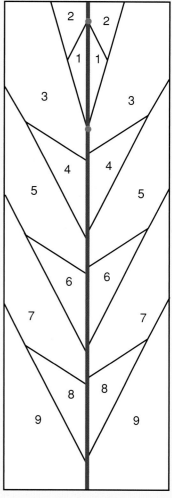

Seam Line Diagram

Note: Unit B is offset from unit A.

1. Make one each of units A and B.

2. Sew unit A to unit B, matching at dots for assembly.

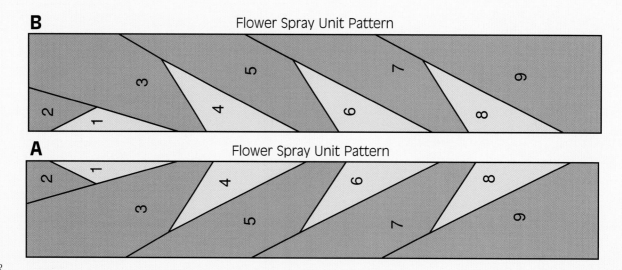

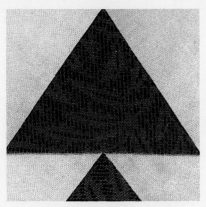

LITTLE TREE
2" block (easy)

Note: This block may be made as a 4" block by joining four blocks.

1. Make one unit A.

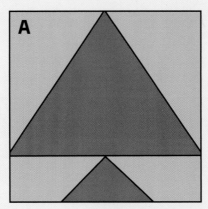

Unit Placement Diagram

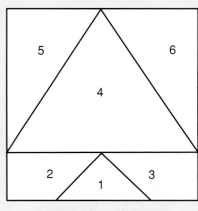

Seam Line Diagram

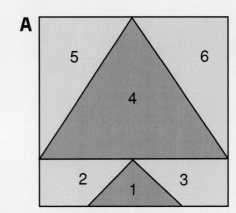

Little Tree Unit Pattern

FERN
2" block (easy)

Note: This block may be made as a 4" block by joining four blocks.

1. Make one unit A.

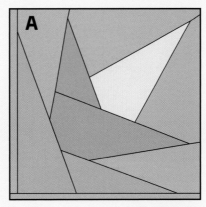

Unit Placement Diagram

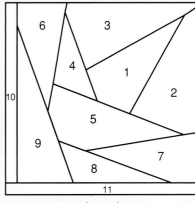

Seam Line Diagram

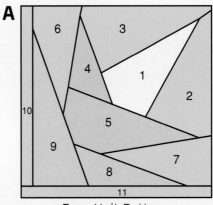

Fern Unit Pattern

MOUSEY
2" x 6" block (moderate)

1. Make one each of units A, B, C, and D.

2. Sew units together in alphabetical order, matching at dots for assembly.

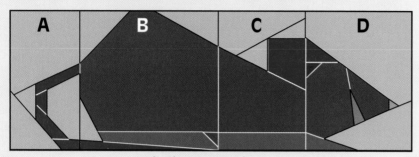

Unit Placement Diagram

B Mousey Unit Pattern

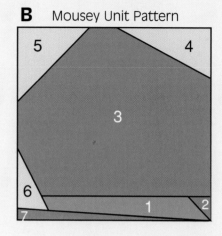

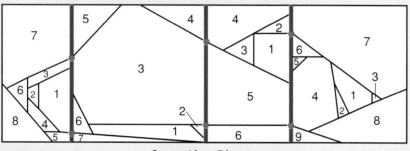

Seam Line Diagram

D Mousey Unit Pattern

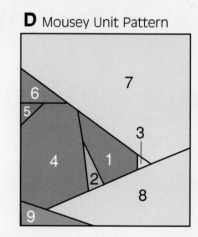

C Mousey Unit Pattern

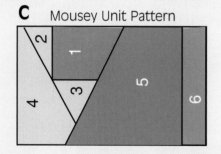

A Mousey Unit Pattern

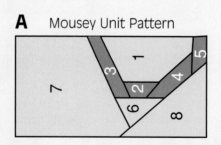

A Artichoke Unit Pattern

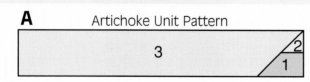

B Artichoke Unit Pattern

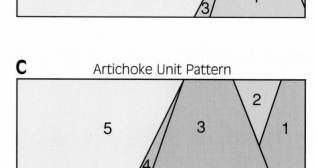

E Artichoke Unit Pattern

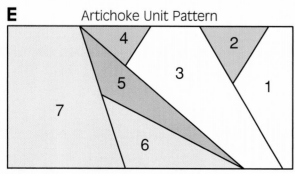

C Artichoke Unit Pattern

ARTICHOKE
6" block (difficult)

1. Make one each of units A, B, C, D, E, F, and G. Make one mirror image each of units A, B, C, D, and E.

2. Sew each unit to its mirror image, matching at dots for assembly.

3. Sew unit F to unit G, matching at dots for assembly.

4. Sew all units together in alphabetical order, matching at dots for assembly.

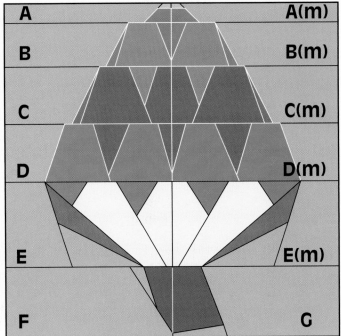

Unit Placement Diagram

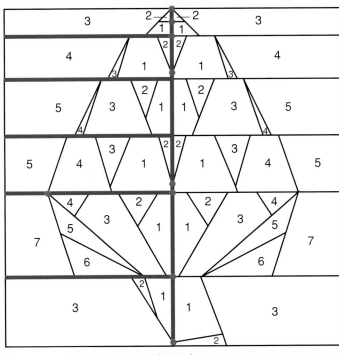

Seam Line Diagram

D   Artichoke Unit Pattern

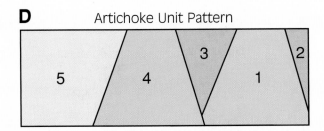

F   Artichoke Unit Pattern

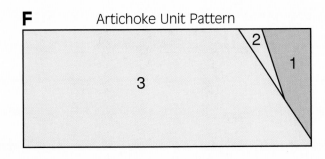

G   Artichoke Unit Pattern

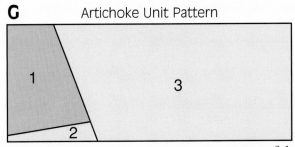

Chapter 3

Garden Tea Party

Just one example of many quilt possibilities.

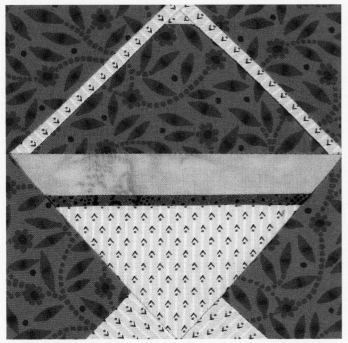

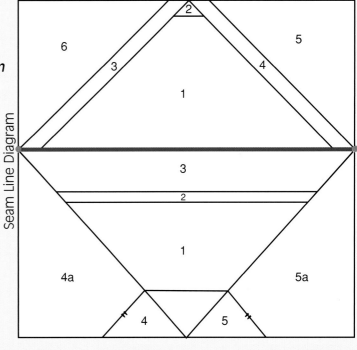

Unit Placement Diagram

FLOWER BASKET
4" block (easy)

Note: Pieces 4 and 4a, and 5 and 5a are preseamed before sewing to unit B. See preseam instructions on page 8.

1. Make one each of units A and B.

2. Sew unit A to unit B, matching at dots for assembly.

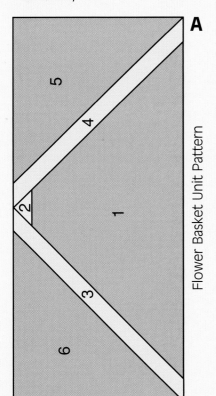

Flower Basket Unit Pattern

Seam Line Diagram

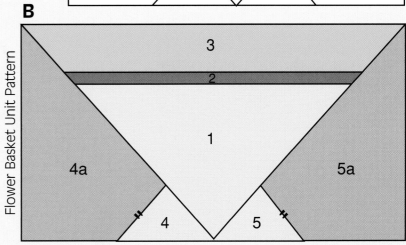

Flower Basket Unit Pattern

F L O W E R   B O U Q U E T
4" block (moderate)

Note: Pieces 6 and 6a are preseamed before sewing to each unit A and mirror image unit A(m). See preseam instructions on page 8.

1. Make one each of units A and B. Make one mirror image of unit A.

2. Sew unit A to mirror image unit A(m), matching at dots for assembly.

3. Clip unit B to seam line at center dots. Sew unit B to unit A–A(m), matching at dots for assembly.

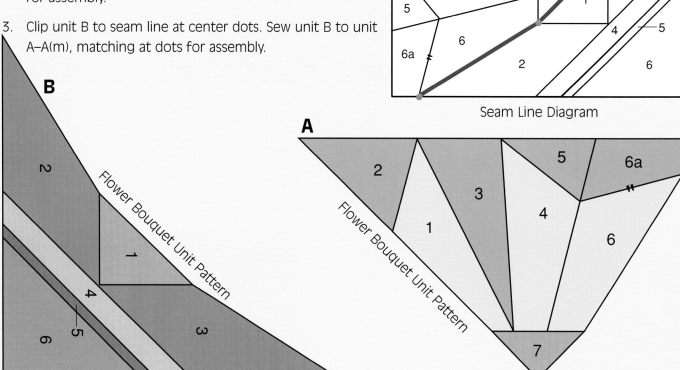

Unit Placement Diagram

Seam Line Diagram

B

Flower Bouquet Unit Pattern

A

Flower Bouquet Unit Pattern

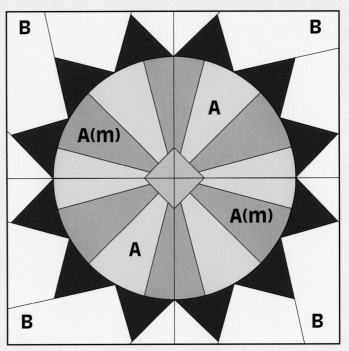

Unit Placement Diagram

WHEEL OF FORTUNE
8" block (moderate)

1. Make two of unit A. Make four of unit B. Make two mirror images of unit A.

2. Cut close to seam line along curved edge of each unit B.

3. Sew each unit A to a unit B, matching at dots for assembly. Repeat for each mirror image unit A(m).

4. Sew each unit A–B to a unit A(m)–B, matching at dots for assembly.

5. Sew units together, matching at dots for assembly.

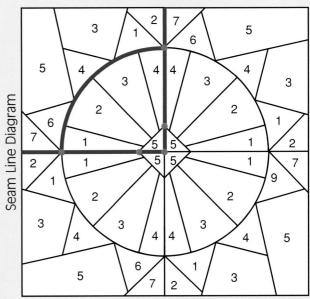

Seam Line Diagram

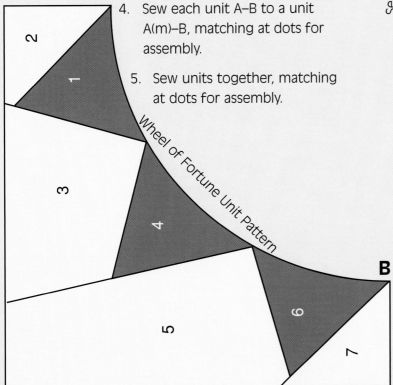

Wheel of Fortune Unit Pattern

B

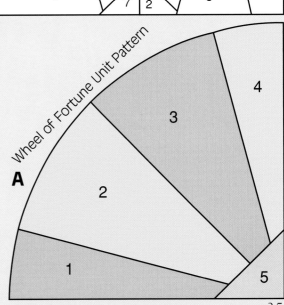

Wheel of Fortune Unit Pattern

A

BLUEBIRD
4" block (moderate)

Note: Pieces 7 and 7a are preseamed before sewing to unit C. See preseam instructions on page 8.

1. Make one each of units A, B, and C.

2. Sew units together in alphabetical order, matching at dots for assembly.

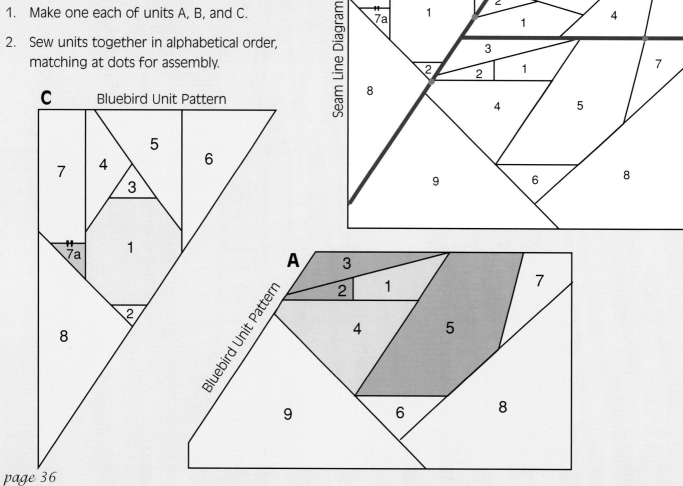

C   Bluebird Unit Pattern

Unit Placement Diagram

Seam Line Diagram

A   Bluebird Unit Pattern

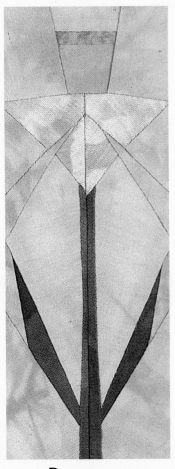

Daffodil

2" x 6" block (moderate)

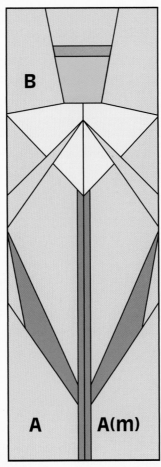

Unit Placement Diagram

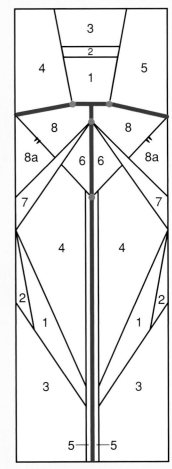

Seam Line Diagram

Note: Pieces 8 and 8a are preseamed before sewing to unit A and mirror image unit A(m). See preseam instructions on page 8.

1. Make one each of units A and B. Make one mirror image of unit A.

2. Sew unit A to mirror image unit A(m), matching at dot for assembly.

3. Clip unit B to seam line at center dots. Sew unit B to unit A–A(m), matching at dots for assembly.

Daffodil Unit Pattern

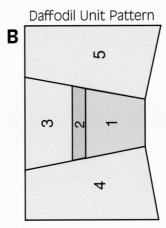

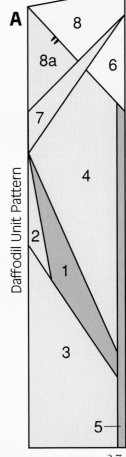

Daffodil Unit Pattern

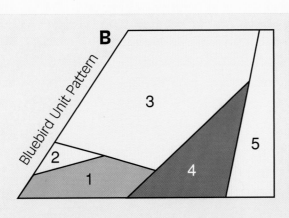

Bluebird Unit Pattern

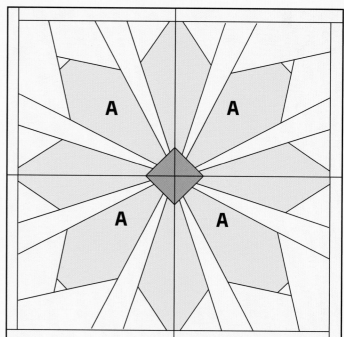

Unit Placement Diagram

Daisy
6" block (moderate)

Note: Pieces 7 and 7a, and 8 and 8a are preseamed before sewing to each unit A. See preseam instructions on page 8.

1. Make four of unit A.

2. Sew four units A together, matching at dots for assembly.

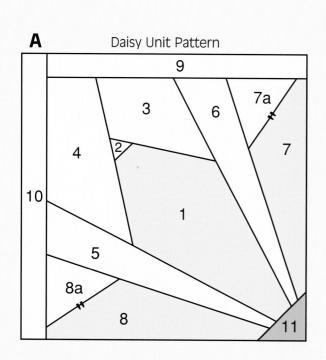

A   Daisy Unit Pattern

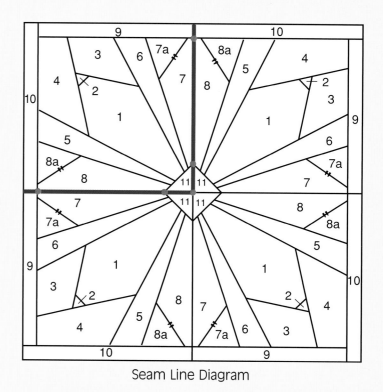

Seam Line Diagram

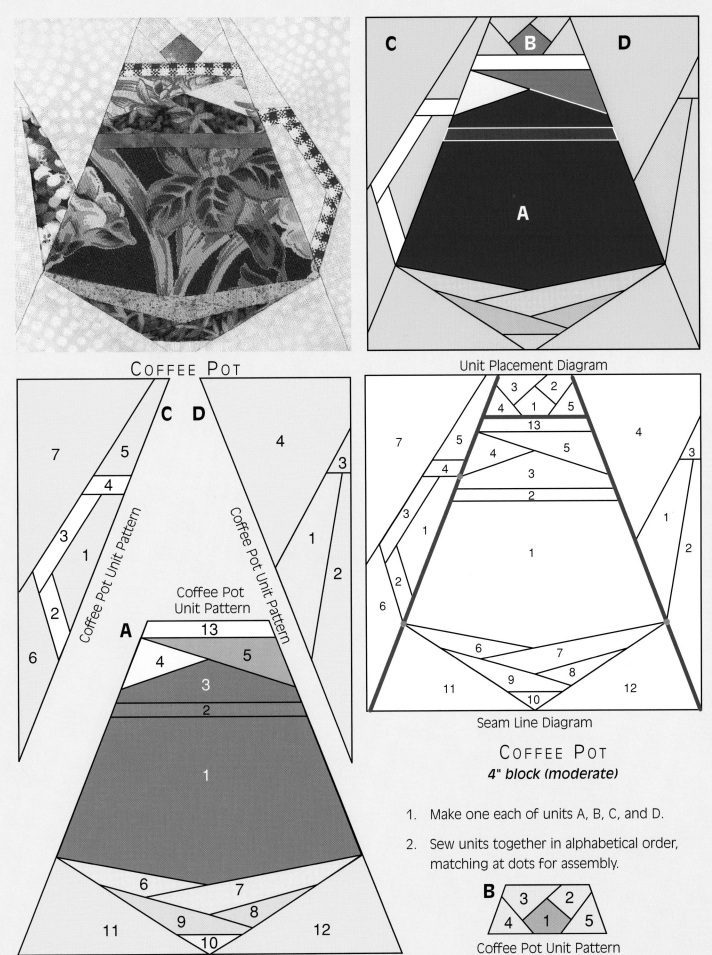

COFFEE POT

C D

7   5

Coffee Pot Unit Pattern

4

4

3

1

3

2

6

Coffee Pot Unit Pattern

Coffee Pot
Unit Pattern

A

13

4

5

3

2

1

6   7

8

9

11   10   12

Unit Placement Diagram

3   2

4   1   5

13

7   5   4

4   3   5

3   2

3   1

1   1

2   2

6

6   7

9   8

11   10   12

Seam Line Diagram

COFFEE POT
4" block (moderate)

1. Make one each of units A, B, C, and D.

2. Sew units together in alphabetical order,
    matching at dots for assembly.

B   3   2
     4   1   5

Coffee Pot Unit Pattern

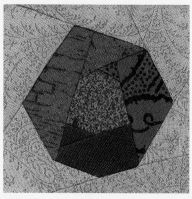

ROSE
2" block (easy)

1. Make one unit A.

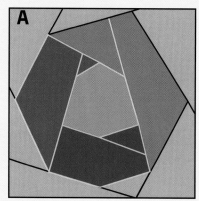

Unit Placement Diagram

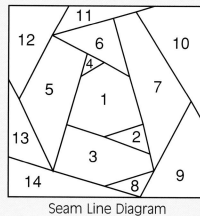

Seam Line Diagram

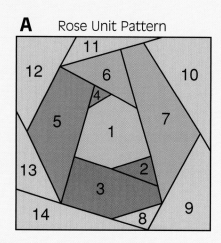

A Rose Unit Pattern

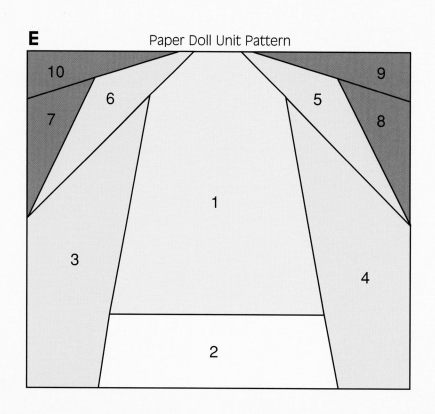

E Paper Doll Unit Pattern

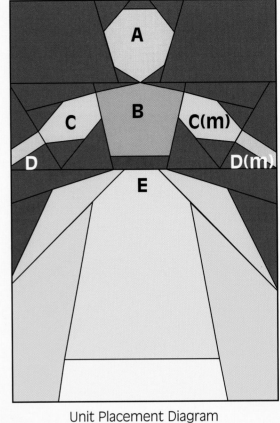

Unit Placement Diagram

PAPER DOLL
4" x 6" block (moderate)

1. Make one each of units A, B, C, D, and E. Make one mirror image each of units C and D.

2. Sew unit C and mirror image unit C(m) to sides of unit B, matching at dots for assembly.

3. Sew unit D and mirror image unit D(m) to sides of unit C–B–C(m), matching at dots for assembly.

4. Sew units A and E to unit D–C–B–C(m)–D(m), matching at dots for assembly.

B Paper Doll
Unit Pattern

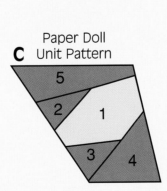

C Paper Doll
Unit Pattern

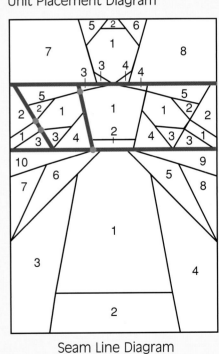

Seam Line Diagram

D Paper Doll Unit Pattern

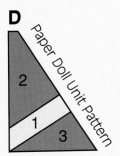

A Paper Doll Unit Pattern

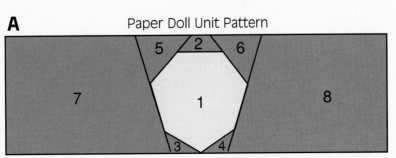

Chapter 4

Dutch Summer

Just one example of many quilt possibilities.

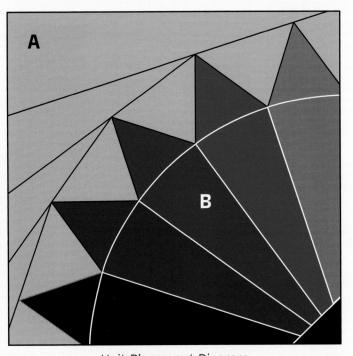

BACHELOR BUTTON
4" block (moderate)

1. Make one each of units A and B.

2. Cut close to seam line along curved edge of unit A.

3. Sew unit A to unit B, matching at dots for assembly.

Unit Placement Diagram

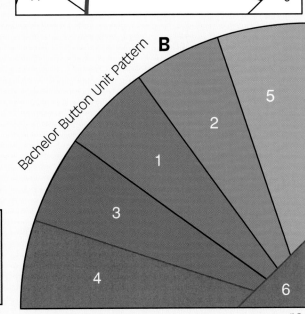

Seam Line Diagram

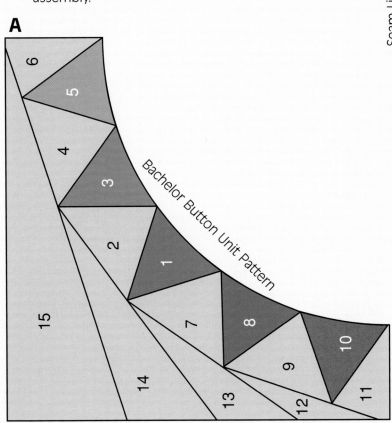

A

Bachelor Button Unit Pattern

B

Bachelor Button Unit Pattern

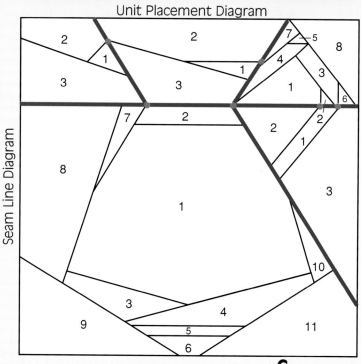

PITCHER
4" block (moderate)

1. Make one each of units A, B, C, D, and E.

2. Sew units A, B, C together in alphabetical order, matching at dots for assembly.

3. Sew unit D to unit E.

4. Sew unit A–B–C to unit D–E, matching at dots for assembly.

Unit Placement Diagram

Seam Line Diagram

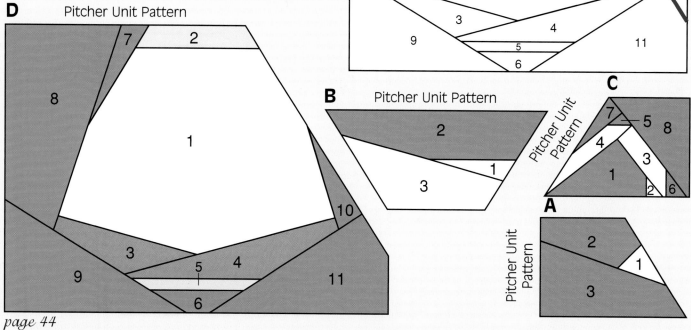

D Pitcher Unit Pattern

B Pitcher Unit Pattern

C Pitcher Unit Pattern

A Pitcher Unit Pattern

TOPIARY
2" x 6" block
(moderate)

1. Make one each of units A, B, and C.

2. Sew units together in alphabetical order, matching at dots for assembly.

3. Sew brown silk ribbon to block for tree trunk.

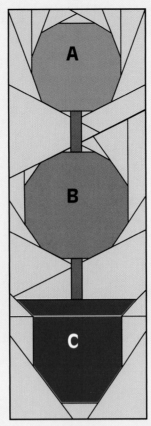

Unit Placement
Diagram

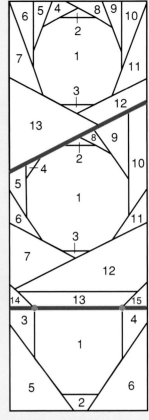

Seam Line Diagram

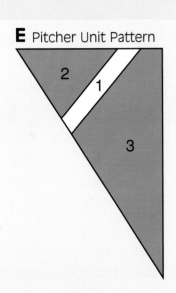

E Pitcher Unit Pattern

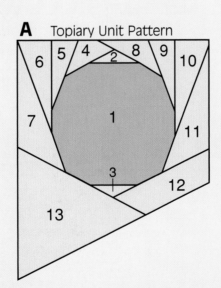

A Topiary Unit Pattern

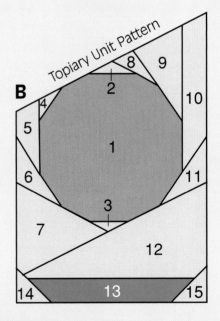

B Topiary Unit Pattern

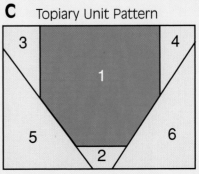

C Topiary Unit Pattern

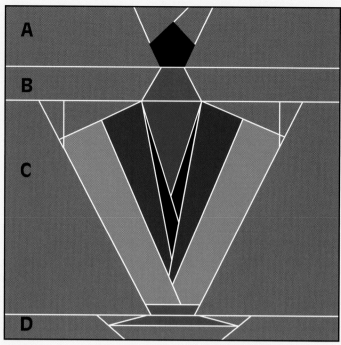

Unit Placement Diagram

PERFUME BOTTLE
4" block (moderate)

1. Make one each of units A, B, C, and D.

2. Sew units together in alphabetical order, matching at dots for assembly.

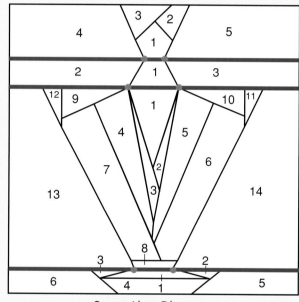

Seam Line Diagram
Perfume Bottle Unit Pattern

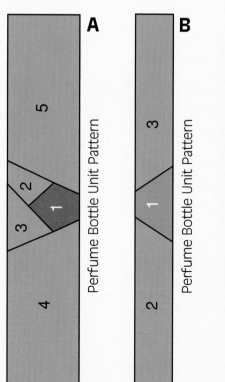

A

Perfume Bottle Unit Pattern

B

Perfume Bottle Unit Pattern

D

Perfume Bottle Unit Pattern

C

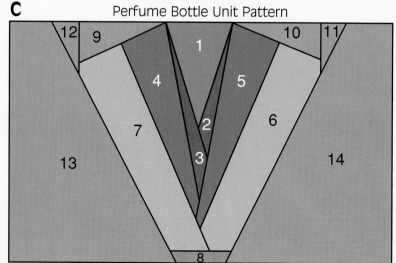

WINDMILL
4" block (moderate)

Note: Pieces 4 and 4a are preseamed before sewing to unit B. See preseam instructions on page 8.

1. Make one each of units A and B. Make one mirror image of unit B.

2. Sew unit B to mirror image unit B(m), matching at dots for assembly. End seam at dot.

3. Sew unit A to unit B–B(m), matching at dots for assembly.

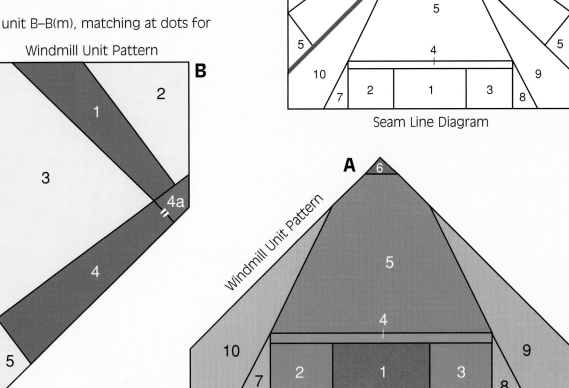

Unit Placement Diagram

Seam Line Diagram

Windmill Unit Pattern

FROND

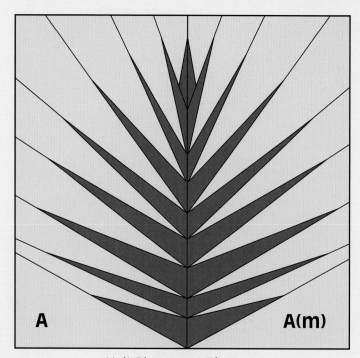

A   **A(m)**

Unit Placement Diagram

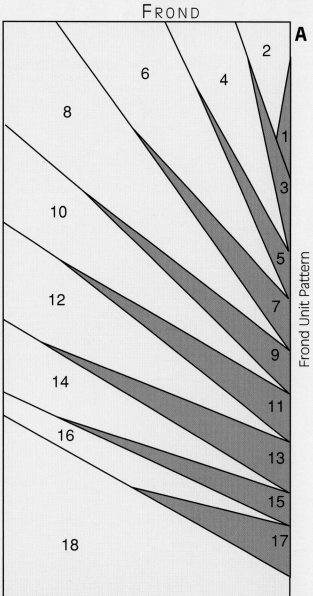

A

Frond Unit Pattern

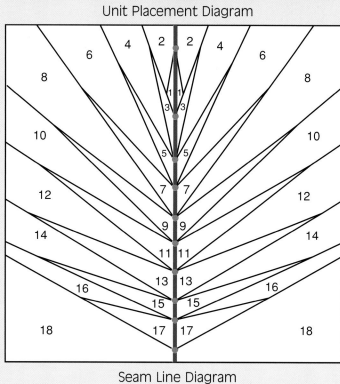

Seam Line Diagram

FROND
6" block (moderate)

1. Make one unit A. Make one mirror image of unit A.

2. Sew unit A to mirror image unit A(m), matching at dots for assembly.

Ivy

4" block (moderate)

Pieces 8 and 8a, and 9 and 9a are preseamed before sewing to unit A. See preseam instructions on page 8.

1. Make one each of units A and B. Make one mirror image of unit B.

2. Sew unit B to mirror image unit B(m), matching at dots for assembly. End seam at dot.

3. Sew unit A to unit B–B(m), matching at dot for assembly.

Unit Placement Diagram

Seam Line Diagram

Ivy Unit Pattern

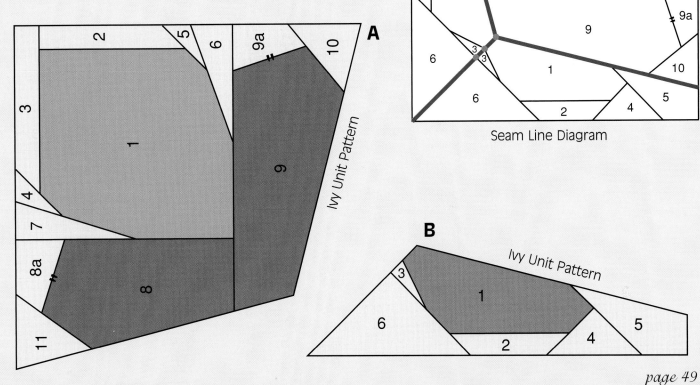

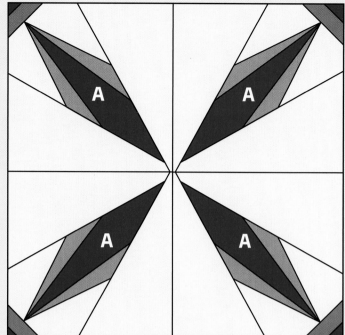

Unit Placement Diagram

TRELLIS
4" block (moderate)

Note: This block may be made as an 8" block by joining four blocks.

1. Make four of unit A.

2. Sew four units A together, matching at dot for assembly.

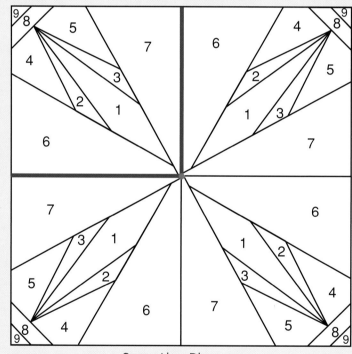

Seam Line Diagram

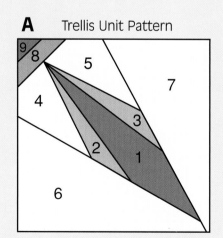

A   Trellis Unit Pattern

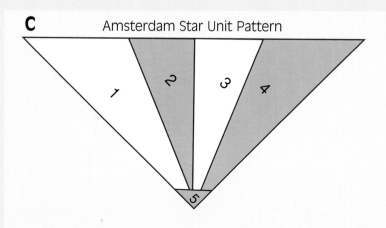

C   Amsterdam Star Unit Pattern

AMSTERDAM STAR
8" block (moderate)

1. Make four each of units A, B, and C.

2. Sew each unit A to a unit B, matching at dot for assembly.

3. Sew each unit C to a unit A–B, matching at dots for assembly.

4. Sew four units A–B–C together, matching at dots for assembly.

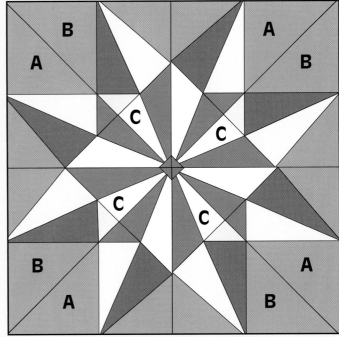

Unit Placement Diagram

Seam Line Diagram

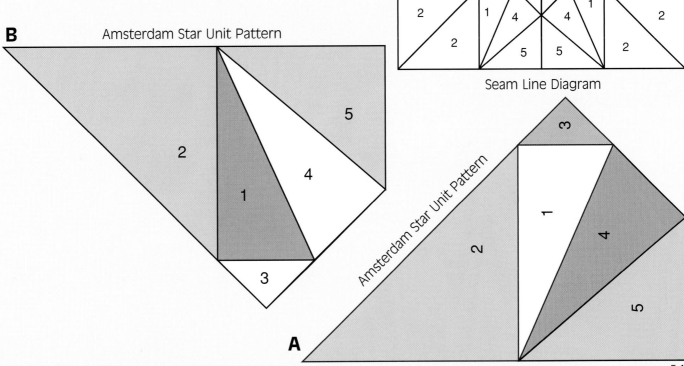

Amsterdam Star Unit Pattern

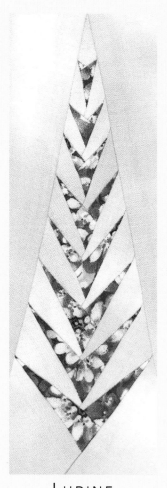

LUPINE
2" x 6" block
(moderate)

1. Make one unit A.

Unit Placement
Diagram

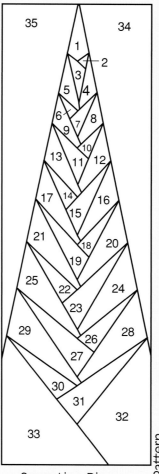

Seam Line Diagram

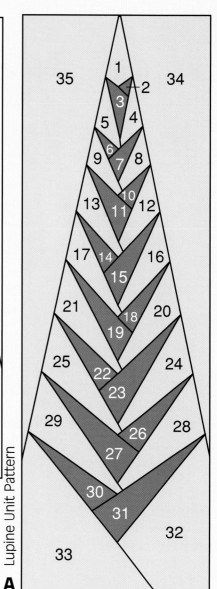

Lupine Unit Pattern

A

MORNING GLORY
2" block (moderate)

1. Make one each of units A and B.

2. Clip unit B to seam line at center. Sew unit A to unit B, matching at dots for assembly.

A

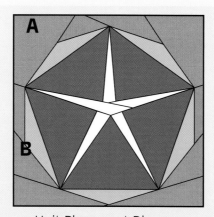

Unit Placement Diagram

Seam Line Diagram

A Morning Glory Unit Pattern

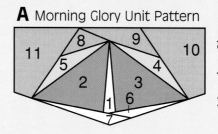

Morning Glory Unit Pattern

B

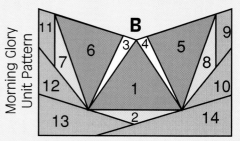

page 52

Chapter 5
A Taste of the Orient

Just one example of many quilt possibilities.

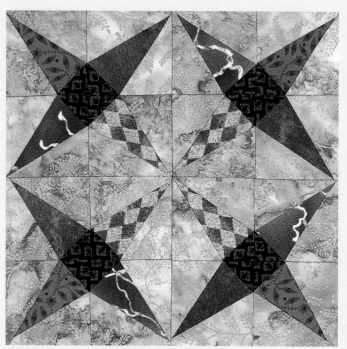

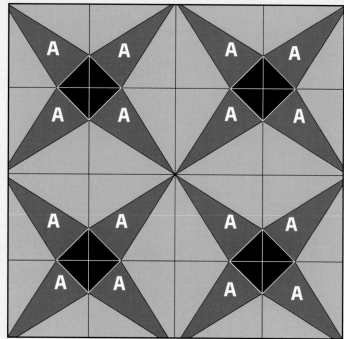

Unit Placement Diagram

SAPPHIRE STAR
8" block (easy)

1. Make sixteen of unit A.

2. Sew four units A together for a 4" block, matching at dots for assembly. Repeat for four 4" blocks.

3. Sew four 4" blocks together, matching at dots for assembly.

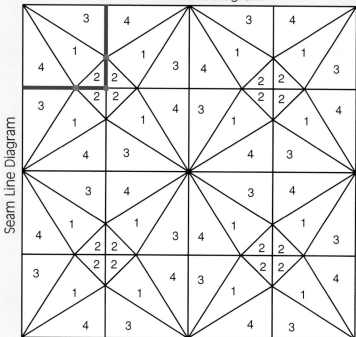

Seam Line Diagram

A Sapphire Star Unit Pattern

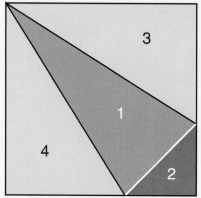

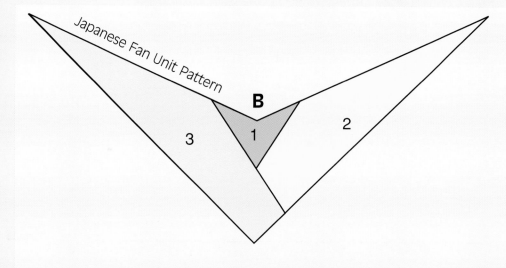

Japanese Fan Unit Pattern

B

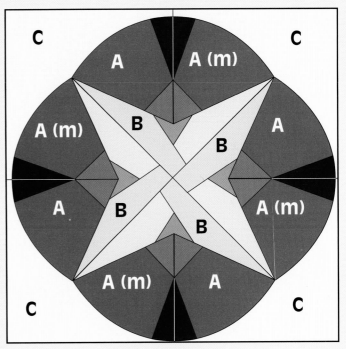

JAPANESE FAN
8" block (difficult)

1. Make four each of units A, B, and C. Make four mirror images of unit A.

2. Sew each unit A to a mirror image unit A(m), matching at dots for assembly.

3. Clip each unit B to seam line at inside dot. Sew each unit B to one unit A–A(m), matching at dots for assembly.

4. Sew four units B–A–A(m) together, matching at dots for assembly.

5. Sew four units C together. Clip curved edge of each unit C slightly. Sew unit A–A(m)–B to unit C, matching curves and seams.

Unit Placement Diagram

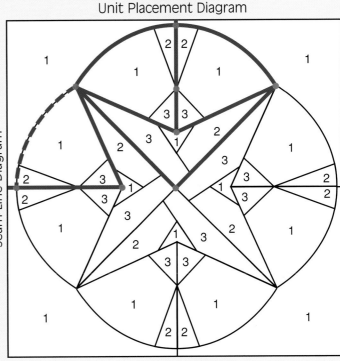

Seam Line Diagram

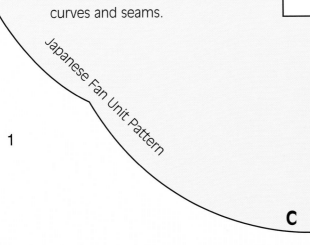

Japanese Fan Unit Pattern

C

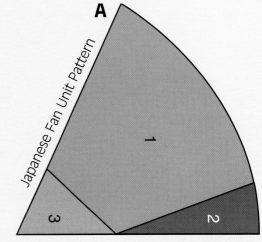

A

Japanese Fan Unit Pattern

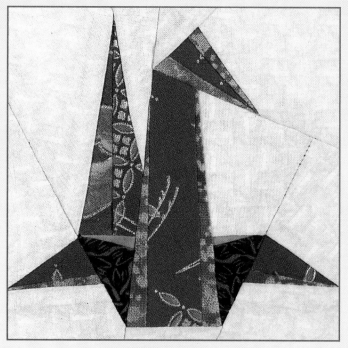

CRANE
4" block (moderate)

1. Make one each of units A, B, C, D, and E.

2. Sew units A, B, and C in alphabetical order, matching at dots for assembly.

3. Sew unit D to unit E, matching at dots for assembly.

4. Sew unit A–B–C to unit D–E, matching at dots for assembly.

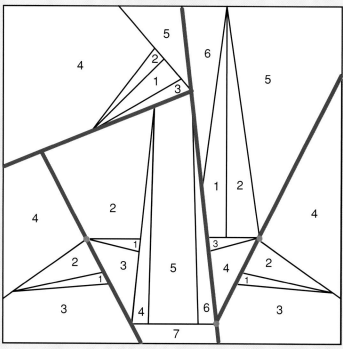

Unit Placement Diagram

Seam Line Diagram

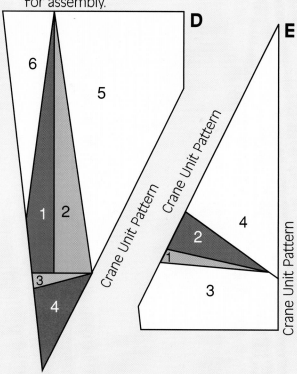

D

E

Crane Unit Pattern

Crane Unit Pattern

Crane Unit Pattern

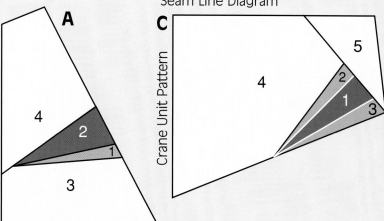

A

C

Crane Unit Pattern

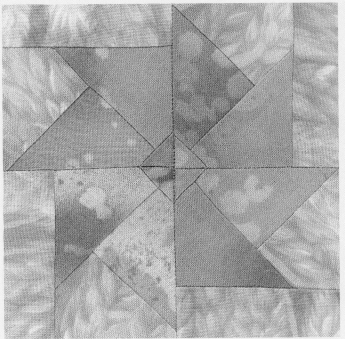

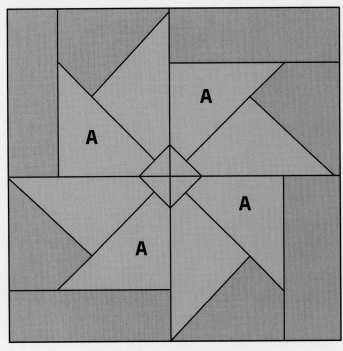

Unit Placement Diagram

P I N W H E E L
4" block (easy)

1. Make four of unit A.

2. Sew four units A together, matching at dots for assembly.

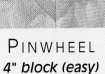

Pinwheel Unit Pattern

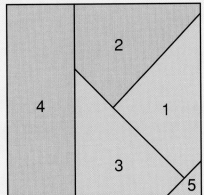

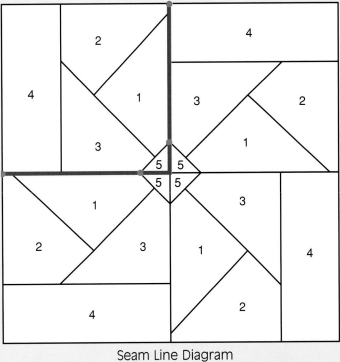

Seam Line Diagram

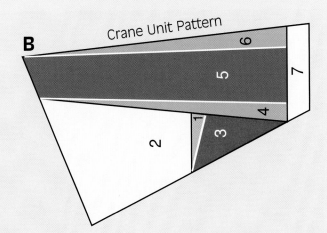

Crane Unit Pattern

KIMONO
4" x 6" block (easy)

1. Make one each of units A and B. Make one mirror image of unit B.

2. Sew unit B and mirror image unit B(m) to each side of unit A.

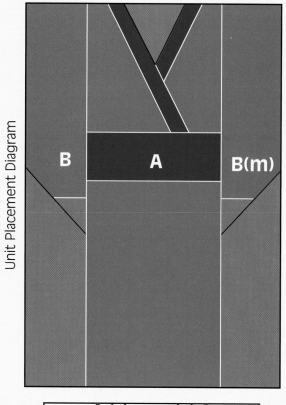

Unit Placement Diagram

B   A   B(m)

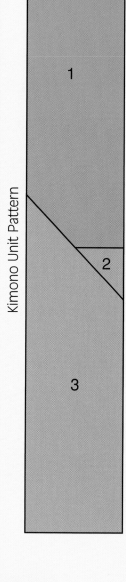

B

1

2

3

Kimono Unit Pattern

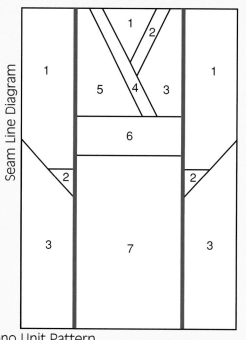

Seam Line Diagram

1   2

1   1

5   4   3

6

2   2

3   7   3

Kimono Unit Pattern

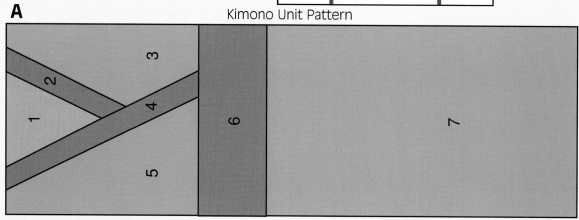

A

1   2   3

5   4

6

7

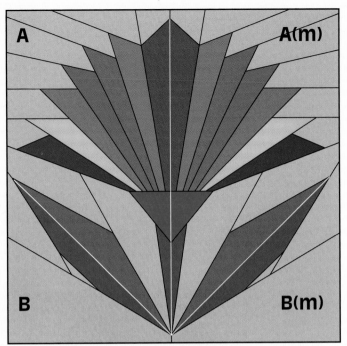

CELESTIAL LOTUS
6" block (moderate)

Pieces 13 and 13a are preseamed before sewing to unit A. See preseam instructions on page 8.

1. Make one each of units A and B. Make one mirror image each of units A and B.

2. Clip unit B to seam line at corner dot. Sew unit A to unit B, matching at dots for assembly. Repeat for mirror image units A(m) and B(m).

3. Sew unit A–B to mirror image unit A(m)–B(m), matching at dots for assembly.

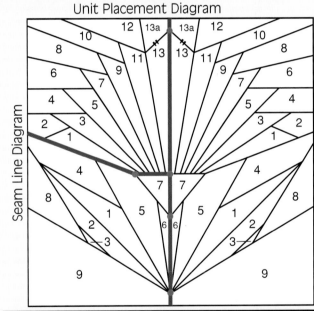

Unit Placement Diagram

Seam Line Diagram

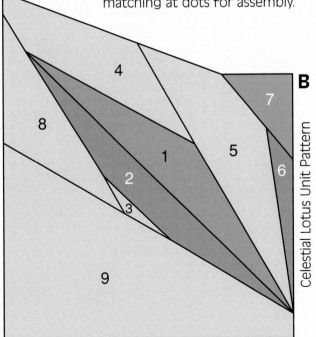

Celestial Lotus Unit Pattern

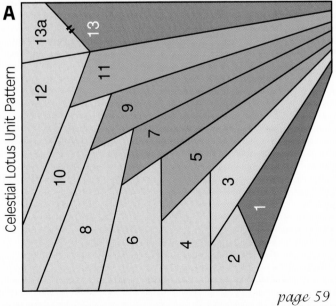

Celestial Lotus Unit Pattern

Chapter 6
Out of Africa

Just one example of many quilt possibilities.

SPIRAL

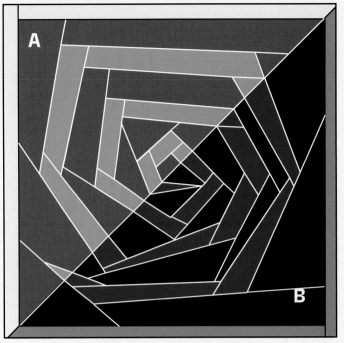

Unit Placement Diagram

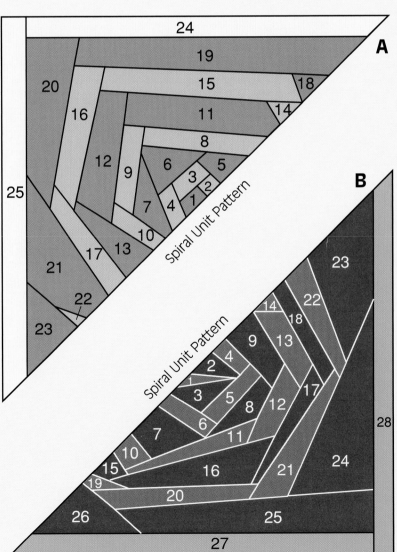

Spiral Unit Pattern

Spiral Unit Pattern

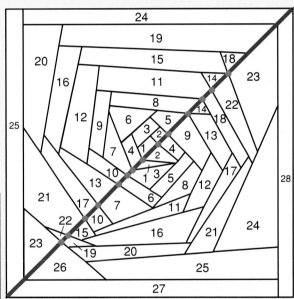

Seam Line Diagram

SPIRAL
4" block (moderate)

1. Make one each of units A and B.

2. Sew unit A to unit B, matching at dots for assembly.

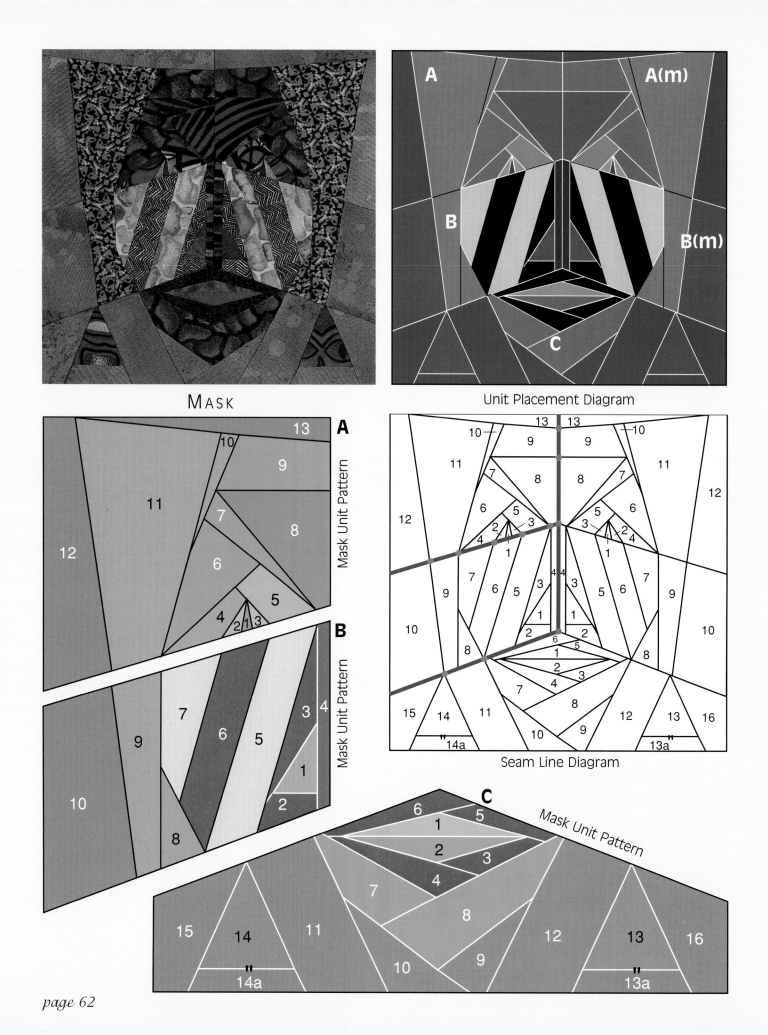

MASK

Unit Placement Diagram

A

Mask Unit Pattern

B

Mask Unit Pattern

Seam Line Diagram

C

Mask Unit Pattern

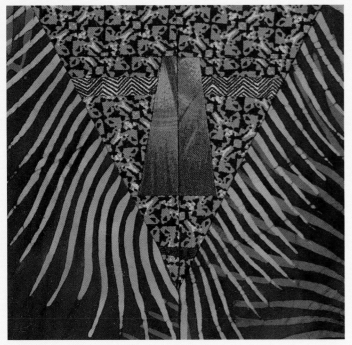

LION
4" block (easy)

1. Make one unit A. Make one mirror image of unit A.

2. Sew unit A to mirror image unit A(m), matching at dots for assembly.

MASK
6" block (moderate)

Note: Pieces 13 and 13a, and 14 and 14a are preseamed before sewing to unit C. See preseam instructions on page 8.

1. Make one each of units A, B, and C. Make one mirror image each of units A and B.

2. Sew unit A to unit B, matching at dots for assembly. Repeat for mirror image units A(m) and B(m).

3. Sew unit A–B to unit A(m)–B(m), matching at dots for assembly. End seam at bottom dot.

4. Sew unit C to bottom of unit A–B–A(m)–B(m), matching at dots for assembly.

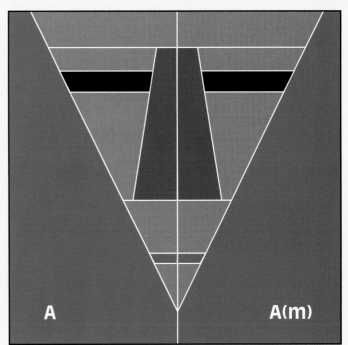

A   **A(m)**

Unit Placement Diagram

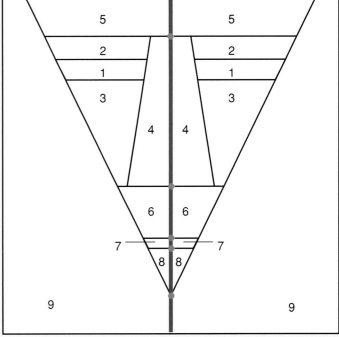

Seam Line Diagram

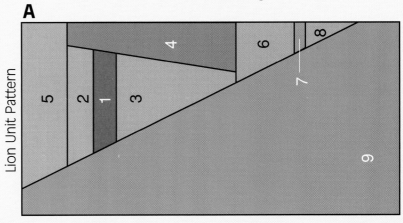

Lion Unit Pattern

FLOWER ORNAMENT
2" x 6" block
(moderate)

1. Make two of unit A. Make one unit B.

2. Sew one unit A to top and one to bottom of unit B, matching at dots for assembly.

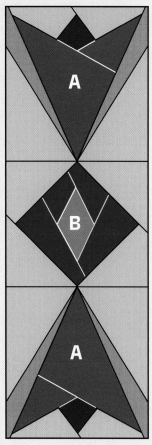

Unit Placement Diagram

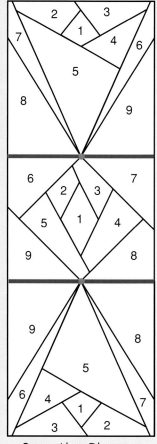

Seam Line Diagram

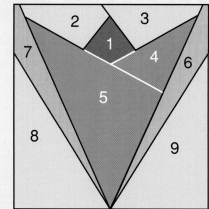

A Flower Ornament Unit Pattern

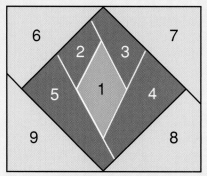

B Flower Ornament Unit Pattern

ANCESTOR
2" x 6" block
(moderate)

1. Make one each of units A, B, and C.

2. Sew units together in alphabetical order, matching at dot for assembly.

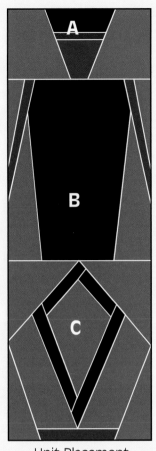

Unit Placement Diagram

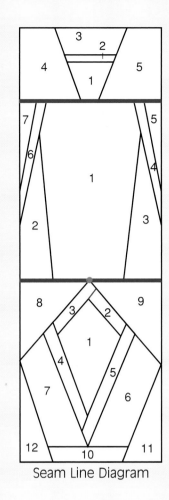

Seam Line Diagram

A Ancestor Unit Pattern

B Ancestor Unit Pattern

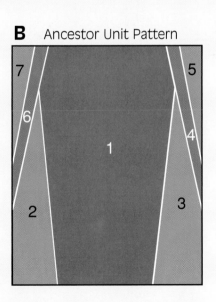

C Ancestor Unit Pattern

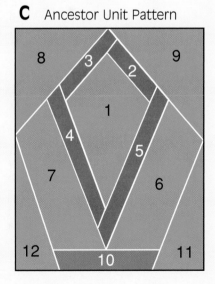

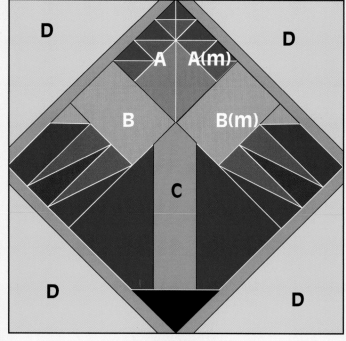

Unit Placement Diagram

TREE OF LIFE
6" block (moderate)

1. Make one each of units A, B, and C. Make four of unit D. Make one mirror image each of units A and B.

2. Sew unit A to mirror image unit A(m), matching at dots for assembly.

3. Sew unit B to unit A–A(m).

4. Sew mirror image unit B(m) to unit C.

5. Sew unit A–A(m)–B to unit B(m)–C, matching at dot for assembly.

6. Sew each unit D to an outer, diagonal edge of unit A–A(m)–B–B(m)–C.

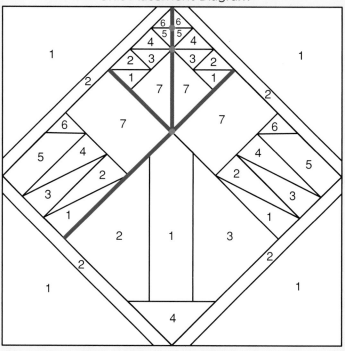

Seam Line Diagram

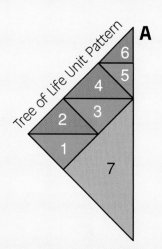

A

Tree of Life Unit Pattern

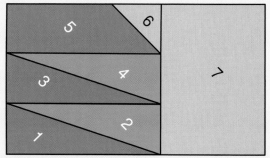

B Tree of Life Unit Pattern

HERRINGBONE
2" block (easy)

1. Make one unit A.

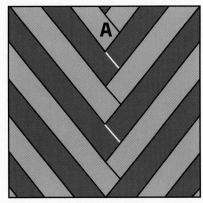

Unit Placement Diagram

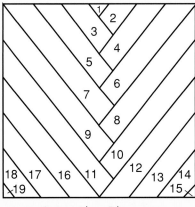

Seam Line Diagram

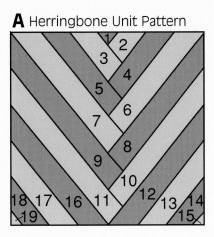

A Herringbone Unit Pattern

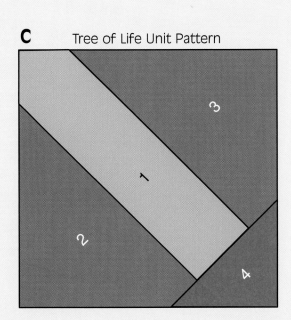

C Tree of Life Unit Pattern

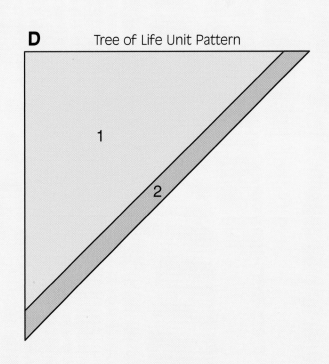

D Tree of Life Unit Pattern

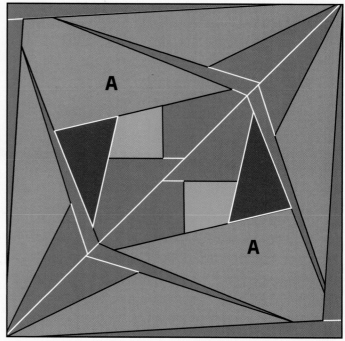

Unit Placement Diagram

AMBER STONE
4" block (moderate)

Pieces 8 and 8a, and 9 and 9a are preseamed before sewing to unit A. See preseam instructions on page 8.

1. Make two of unit A.

2. Sew two units A together, matching at dots for assembly.

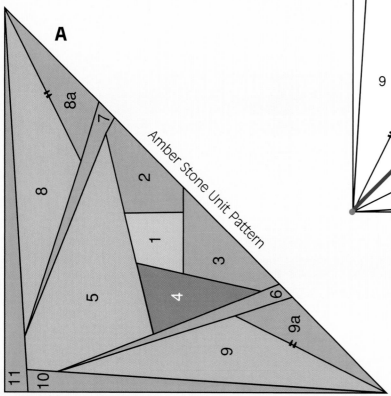

Seam Line Diagram

Chapter 7
A Christmas Vision

Just one example of many quilt possibilities.

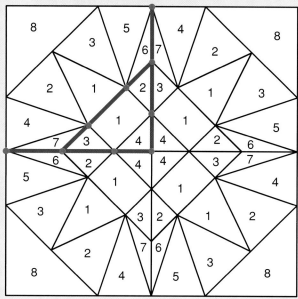

Unit Placement Diagram

NORTH STAR
8" block (moderate)

1. Make four each of units A and B.

2. Sew each unit A to a unit B, matching at dots for assembly.

3. Sew four units A–B together, matching at dots for assembly.

Seam Line Diagram

A North Star Unit Pattern

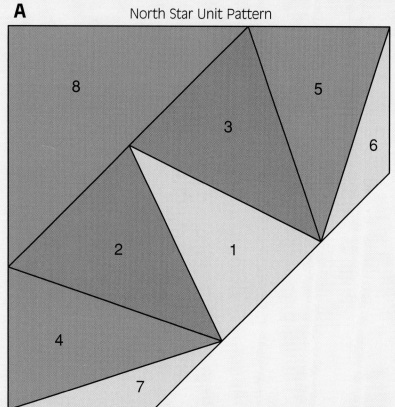

B

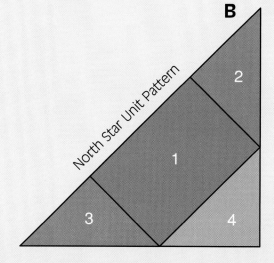

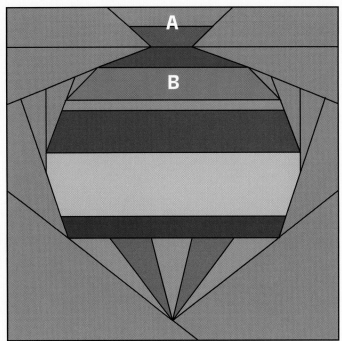

Unit Placement Diagram

ORNAMENT
4" block (moderate)

1. Make one each of units A and B.

2. Sew unit A to unit B, matching at dots for assembly.

B Ornament Unit Pattern

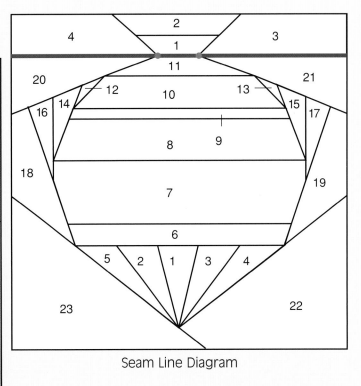

Seam Line Diagram

Ornament Unit Pattern

A

ANGEL
4" block (moderate)

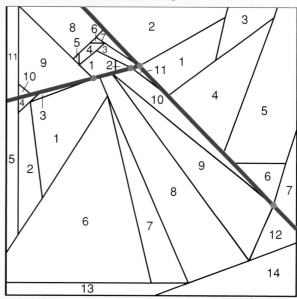

Unit Placement Diagram

1. Make one each of units A, B, and C.

2. Sew unit A to unit B, matching at dots for assembly.

3. Sew unit C to unit A–B, matching at dots for assembly.

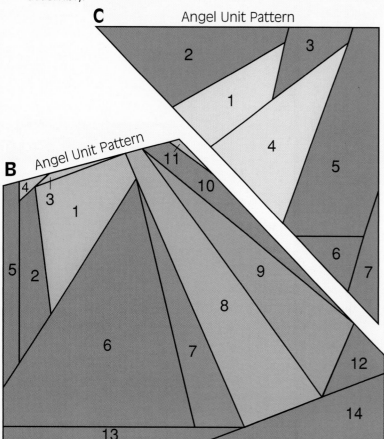

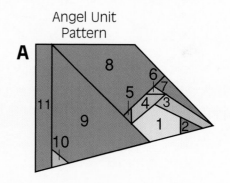

Seam Line Diagram

Angel Unit Pattern

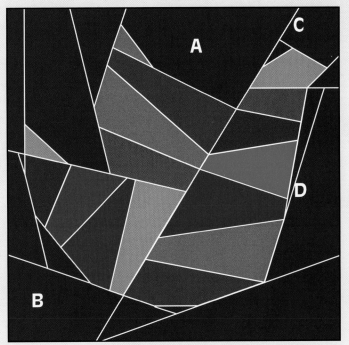

Unit Placement Diagram

DOVE
4" block (moderate)

1. Make one each of units A, B, C, and D.

2. Sew unit A to unit B.

3. Sew unit C to unit D, matching at dots for assembly.

4. Sew unit A–B to unit C–D, matching at dots for assembly.

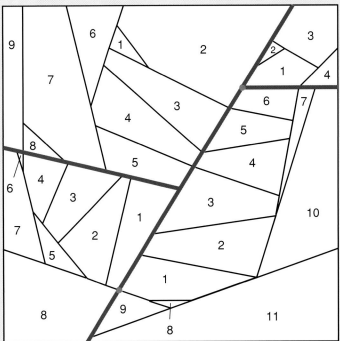

Seam Line Diagram

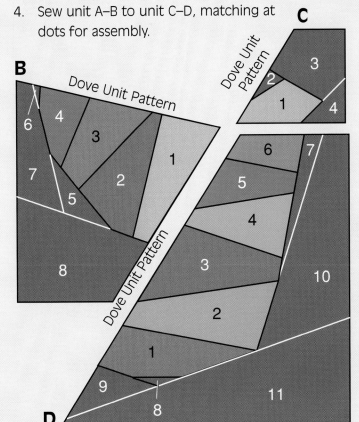

B

Dove Unit Pattern

C

Dove Unit Pattern

D

Dove Unit Pattern

A

Dove Unit Pattern

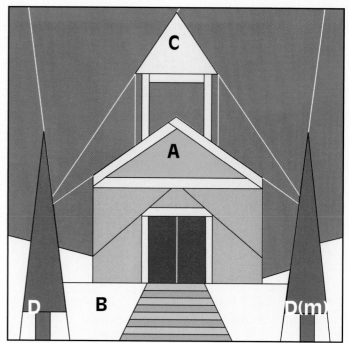

Unit Placement Diagram

COUNTRY CHURCH
6" block (difficult)

Note: Pieces 15 and 15a, and 16 and 16a are preseamed before sewing to unit A. Pieces 5 and 5a are preseamed before sewing to unit D. See preseam instructions on page 8.

1. Make one each of units A, B, C, and D. Make one mirror image of unit D.

2. Clip unit C to seam line at center dot. Sew units A, B, and C together in alphabetical order, matching at dots for assembly.

3. Sew unit D to side of unit A–B–C. Repeat for mirror image unit D(m).

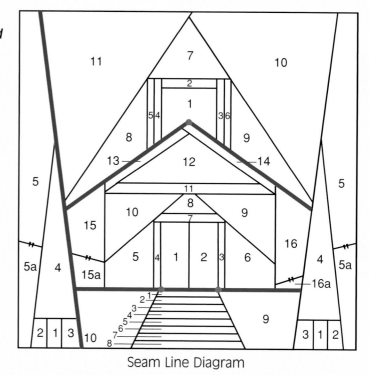

Seam Line Diagram

B Country Church Unit Pattern

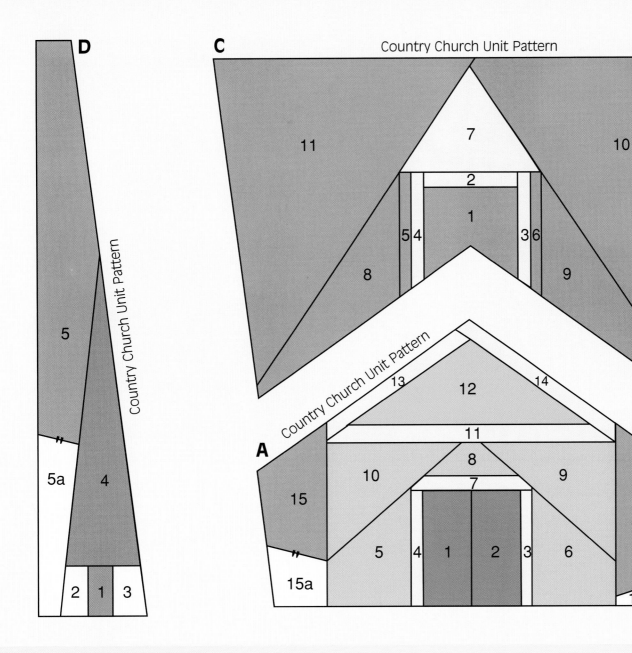

D

Country Church Unit Pattern

C

Country Church Unit Pattern

A

Country Church Unit Pattern

Note: See Nutcracker block on page 76.

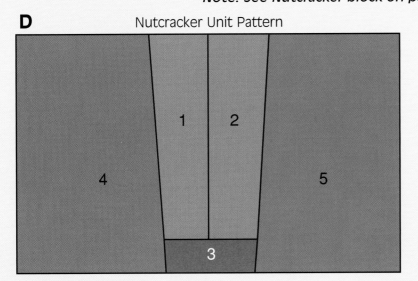

D Nutcracker Unit Pattern

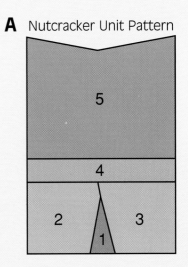

A Nutcracker Unit Pattern

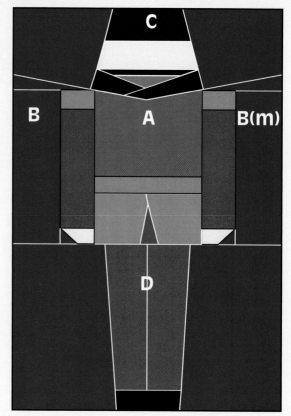

Unit Placement Diagram

NUTCRACKER
4" x 6" block (moderate)

1. Make one each of units A, B, C, and D. Make one mirror image of unit B.

2. Sew unit B and mirror image unit B(m) to sides of unit A.

3. Clip unit A to seam line at dot. Sew unit C to unit B–A–B(m), matching at dot for assembly.

4. Sew unit D to unit C–B–A–B(m), matching at dot for assembly.

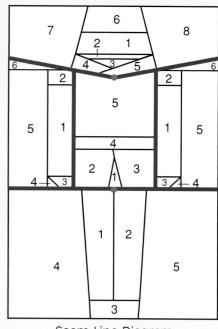

Seam Line Diagram

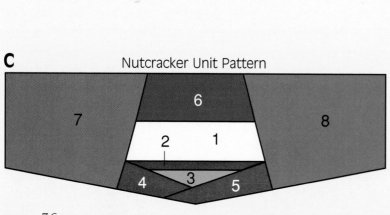

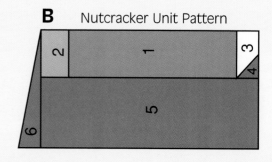

Chapter 8

Up North

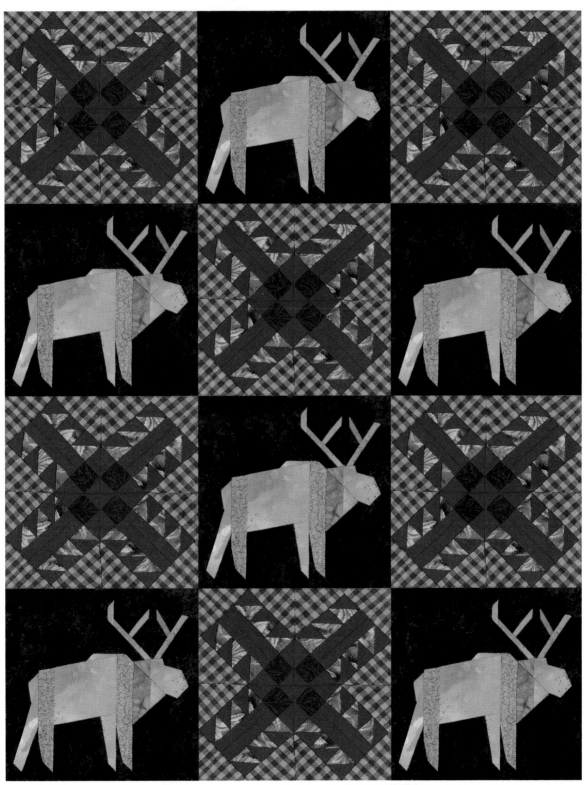

Just one example of many quilt possibilities.

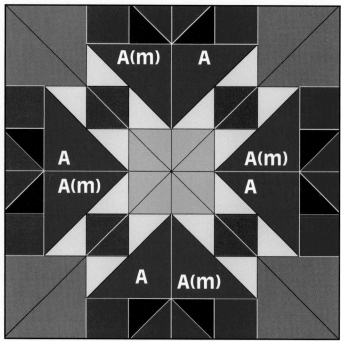

Unit Placement Diagram

CROW'S FOOT
8" block (moderate)

Note: Pieces 6 and 6a are preseamed before sewing to unit A and mirror image unit A(m). See preseam instructions on page 8.

1. Make four of unit A. Make four mirror images of unit A.

2. Sew each unit A to a mirror image unit A(m), matching at dots for assembly.

3. Sew four units A–A(m) together, matching at dots for assembly.

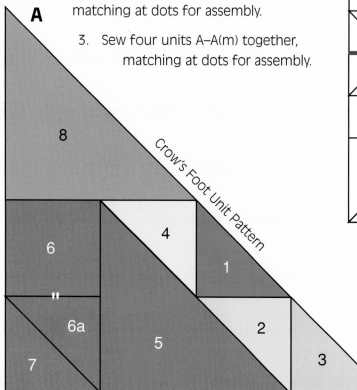

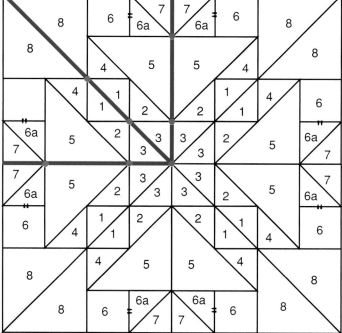

Seam Line Diagram

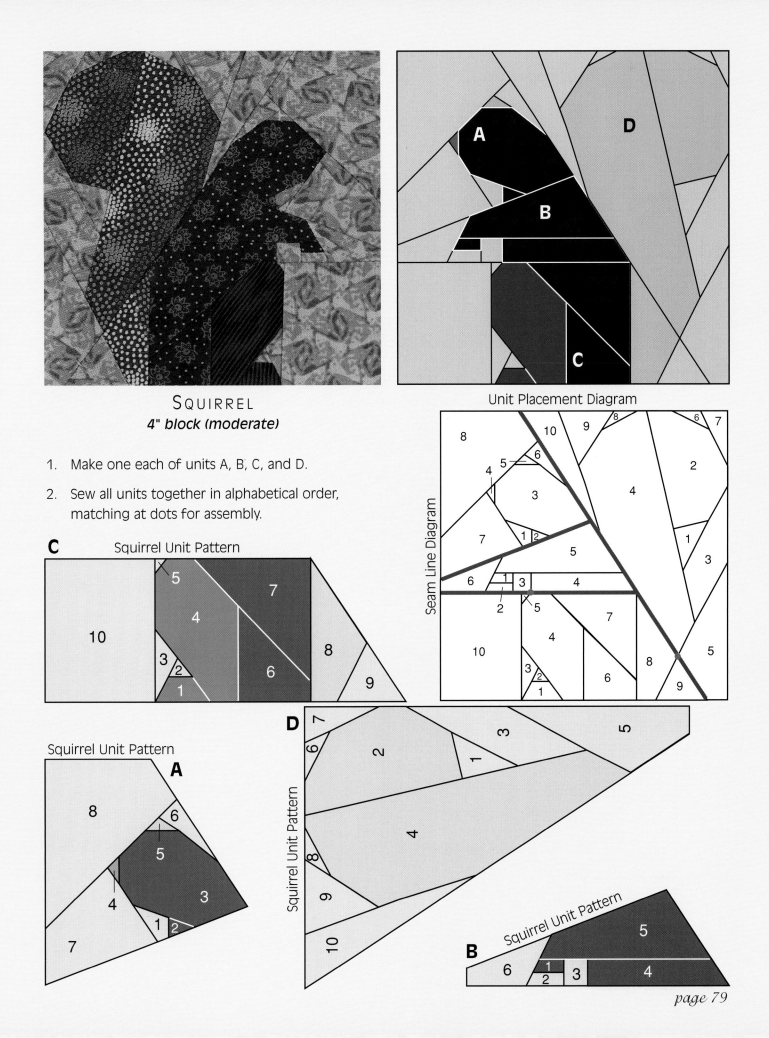

SQUIRREL
4" block (moderate)

1. Make one each of units A, B, C, and D.

2. Sew all units together in alphabetical order, matching at dots for assembly.

Unit Placement Diagram

Seam Line Diagram

C Squirrel Unit Pattern

Squirrel Unit Pattern

A

D Squirrel Unit Pattern

Squirrel Unit Pattern

B

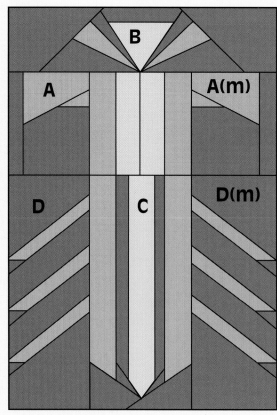

Unit Placement Diagram

1. Make one each of units A, B, C, and D. Make one mirror image each of units A and D.

2. Sew unit A to mirror image unit A(m), matching at dots for assembly.

3. Sew unit B to unit A–A(m), matching at dots for assembly.

4. Sew unit D to side of unit C. Repeat for mirror image unit D(m).

5. Sew unit A–A(m)–B to unit D–C–D(m), matching at dots for assembly.

B

Northern Woods Unit Pattern

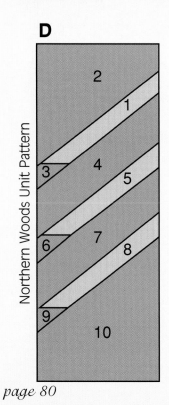

Northern Woods Unit Pattern

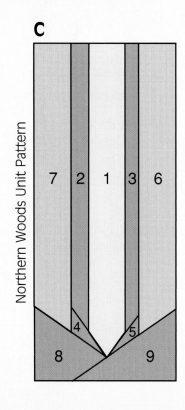

Northern Woods Unit Pattern

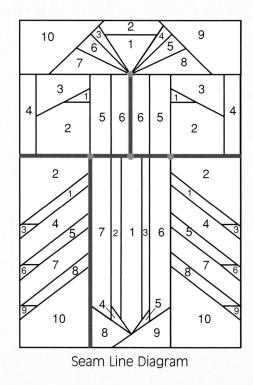

Seam Line Diagram

CROSSROADS
6" block (difficult)

1. Make four each of units A and B. Make four mirror images of unit A.

2. Sew each unit A to a mirror image unit A(m) matching at dot for assembly.

3. Sew each unit B to a unit A–A(m), matching at dots for assembly.

4. Sew four units B–A–A(m) together, matching at dots for assembly.

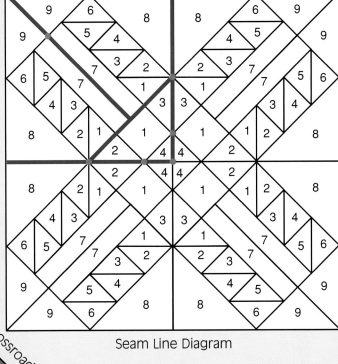

Unit Placement Diagram

Seam Line Diagram

Northern Woods Unit Pattern

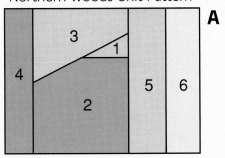

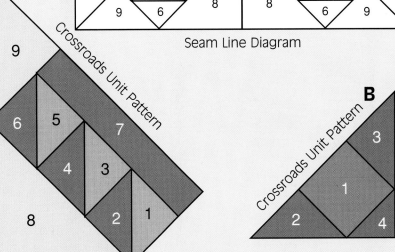

A

Crossroads Unit Pattern

B

Crossroads Unit Pattern

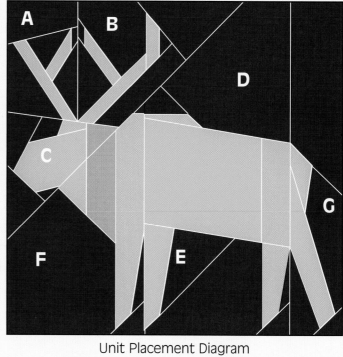

Unit Placement Diagram

ELK
6" block (moderate)

Note: Pieces 4 and 4a are preseamed before sewing to unit D. See preseam instructions on page 8.

1. Make one each of units A, B, C, D, E, F, and G.

2. Sew units A, B, and C together in alphabetical order, matching at dot for assembly.

3. Sew units D, E, F and G together, matching at dots for assembly.

4. Sew unit A–B–C to unit D–E–F–G, matching at dots for assembly.

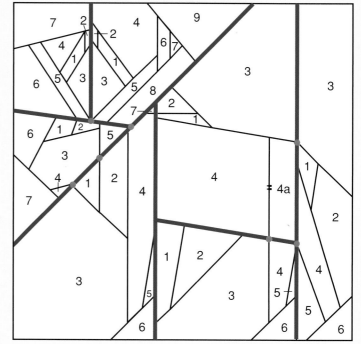

Seam Line Diagram

G

Elk Unit Pattern

E

Elk Unit Pattern

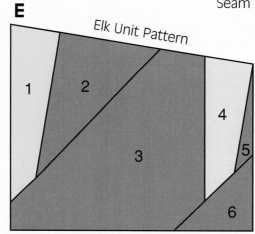

A

Elk Unit Pattern

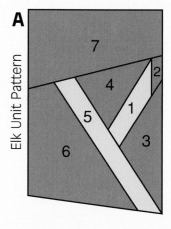

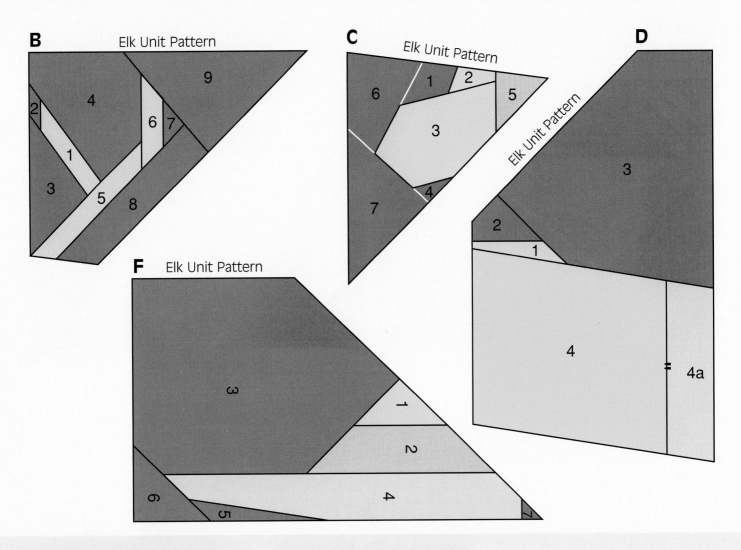

B Elk Unit Pattern

C Elk Unit Pattern

D Elk Unit Pattern

F Elk Unit Pattern

AUTUMN LEAVES
2" block (easy)

1. Make one each of units A and B.

2. Sew unit A to unit B.

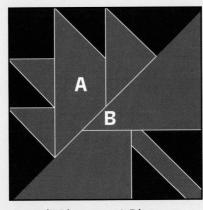

Unit Placement Diagram

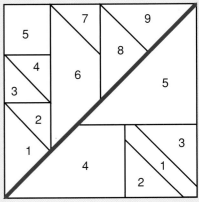

Seam Line Diagram

A Autumn Leaves Unit Pattern

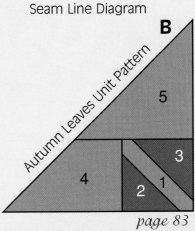

B Autumn Leaves Unit Pattern

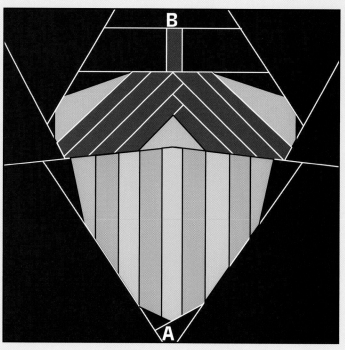

Unit Placement Diagram

Acorn
4" block (moderate)

Note: Pieces 16, 16a, and 16b are preseamed before sewing to unit B. See preseam instructions on page 8.

1. Make one each of units A and B.

2. Clip unit B to seam line at center dot.

3. Sew unit A to unit B, matching at dot for assembly.

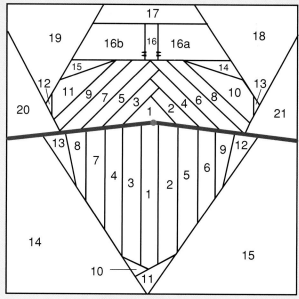

Seam Line Diagram

B

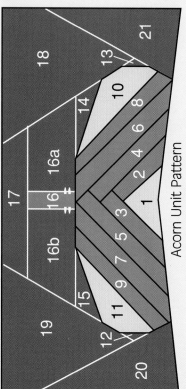

Acorn Unit Pattern

Acorn Unit Pattern

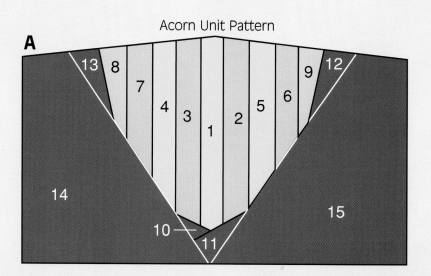

Chapter 9

Spring's Fancy

Just one example of many quilt possibilities.

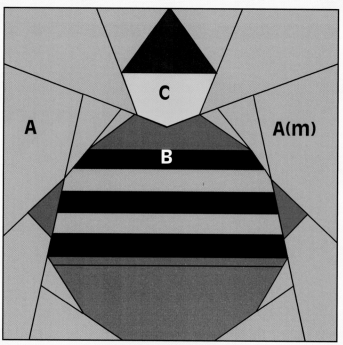

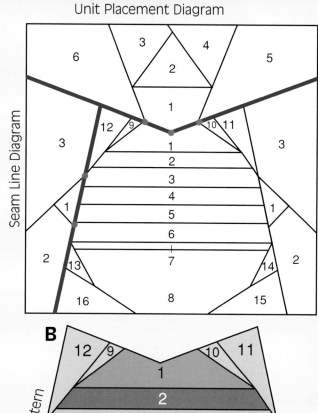

ROLLY POLLY
4" block (moderate)

1. Make one each of units A, B, and C. Make one mirror image of unit A.

2. Sew unit A to side of unit B, matching at dots for assembly. Repeat for mirror image unit A(m).

3. Clip unit B to seam line at center top dot. Sew unit C to unit A–B–A(m), matching at dots for assembly.

Unit Placement Diagram

Seam Line Diagram

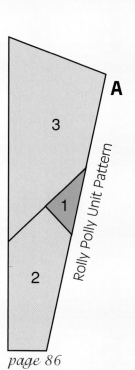

Rolly Polly Unit Pattern

A

3

1

2

C

Rolly Polly Unit Pattern

5

4

2

3

1

6

B

Rolly Polly Unit Pattern

12 9 10 11

1

2

3

4

5

6

13 7 14

16 8 15

EVENING FLOWER
6" block (moderate)

Note: Pieces 4 and 4a, and 5 and 5a are preseamed before sewing to each unit A. See preseam instructions on page 8.

1. Make four each of units A and B.

2. Sew each unit A to a unit B.

3. Sew four units A–B together, matching at dots for assembly.

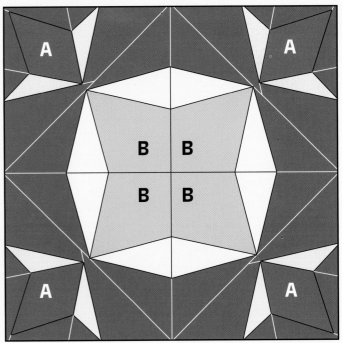

Unit Placement Diagram

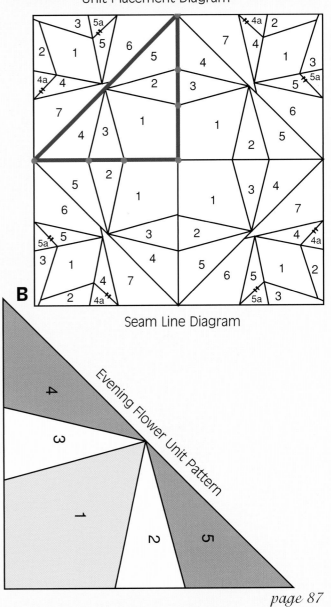

Seam Line Diagram

A Evening Flower Unit Pattern

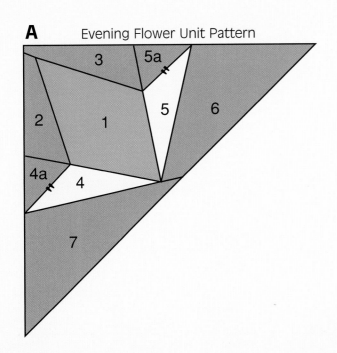

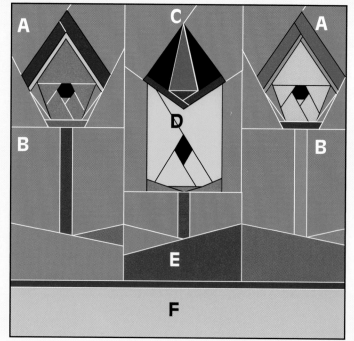

Unit Placement Diagram

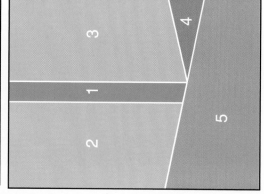

Seam Line Diagram

BIRDHOUSE LANDSCAPE
6" block (difficlut)

1. Make two each of units A and B. Make one each of units C, D, E, and F.

2. Sew each unit A to a unit B.

3. Clip unit D to seam line at center top dot. Sew units C, D, and E together in alphabetical order.

4. Sew a unit A–B to each side of unit C–D–E, matching at dots for assembly.

5. Sew unit F to unit A–B–C–D–E.

C Birdhouse Landscape Unit Pattern

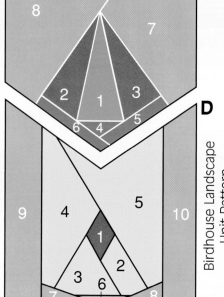

D Birdhouse Landscape Unit Pattern

Birdhouse Landscape Unit Pattern

A Birdhouse Landscape Unit Pattern

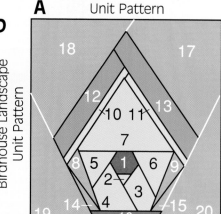

B Birdhouse Landscape Unit Pattern

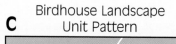

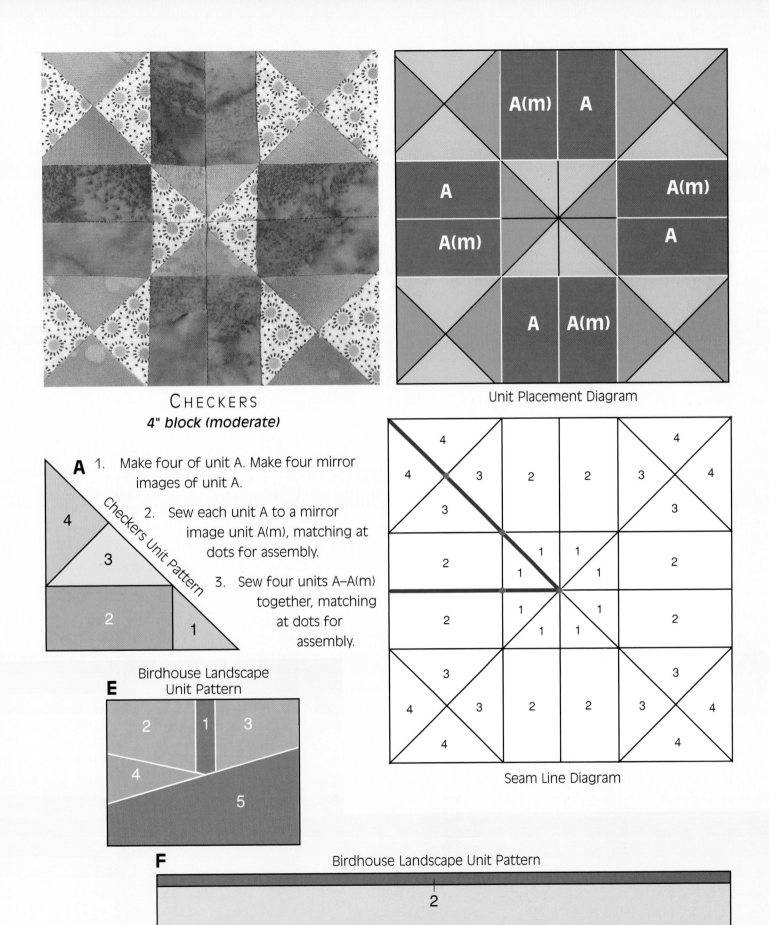

CHECKERS

4" block (moderate)

Unit Placement Diagram

A 1. Make four of unit A. Make four mirror images of unit A.

2. Sew each unit A to a mirror image unit A(m), matching at dots for assembly.

3. Sew four units A–A(m) together, matching at dots for assembly.

Checkers Unit Pattern

Seam Line Diagram

Birdhouse Landscape
Unit Pattern

E

Birdhouse Landscape Unit Pattern

F

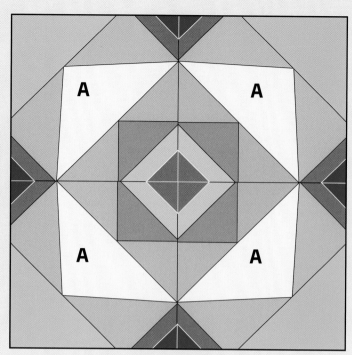

Unit Placement Diagram

SOLOMON'S TEMPLE
8" block (moderate)

1. Make four of unit A.

2. Sew units A together, matching at dots for assembly.

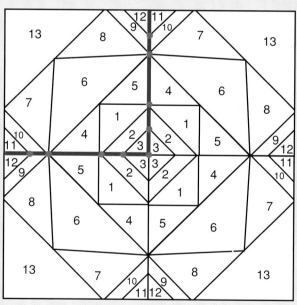

Seam Line Diagram

A Solomon's Temple Unit Pattern

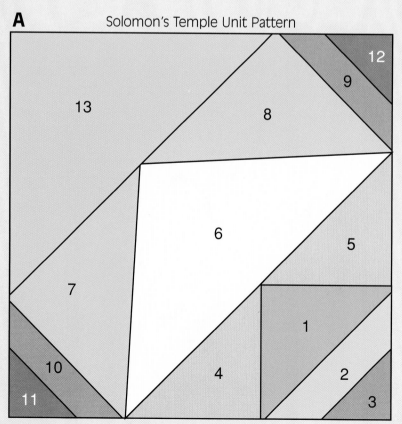

CARNATION
8" block (moderate)

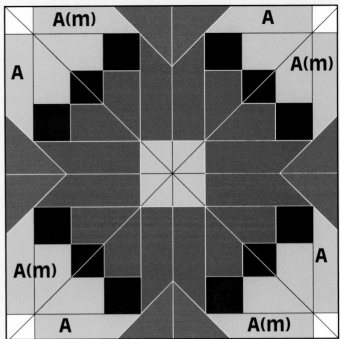

Unit Placement Diagram

Note: Pieces 3 and 3a are preseamed before sewing to each unit A and each mirror image unit A(m). See preseam instructions on page 8.

1. Make four of unit A. Make four mirror images of unit A.

2. Sew each unit A to a mirror image unit A(m), matching at dots for assembly.

3. Sew four units A together, matching at dots for assembly.

Carnation Unit Pattern

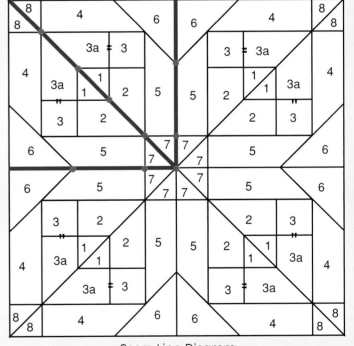

Seam Line Diagram

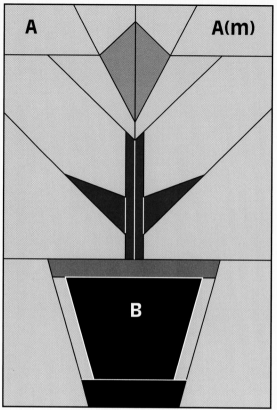

Unit Placement Diagram

FLOWER POT
4" x 6" block
(moderate)

Note: Pieces 7 and 7a are preseamed before sewing to unit A and mirror image unit A(m). See preseam instructions on page 8.

1. Make one each of unit A and B. Make one mirror image of unit A.

2. Sew unit A to mirror image unit A(m), matching at dots for assembly.

3. Sew unit B to unit A–A(m).

A Flower Pot Unit Pattern

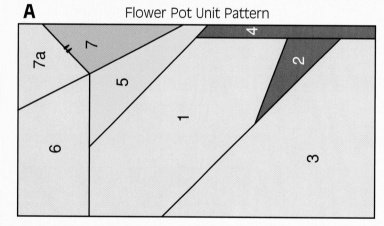

B Flower Pot Unit Pattern

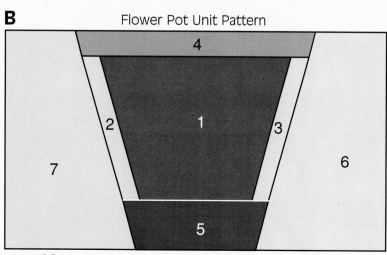

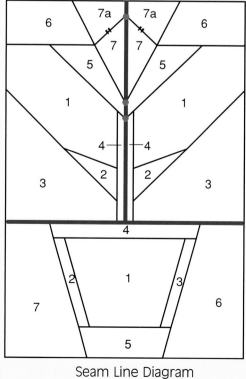

Seam Line Diagram

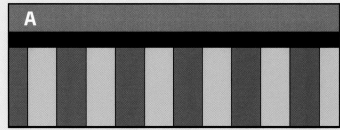

STRIPE
2" x 6" block (easy)

Unit Placement Diagram

1. Make one unit A

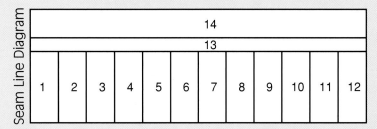

Stripe Unit Pattern

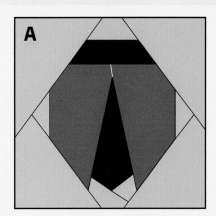

LADYBUG
2" block (easy)

1. Make one unit A.

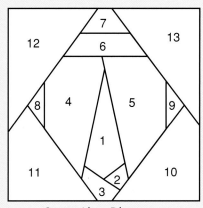

Unit Placement Diagram

Seam Line Diagram

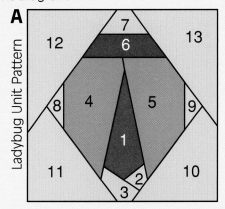

Chapter 10

Sugar & Spice

Just one example of many quilt possibilities.

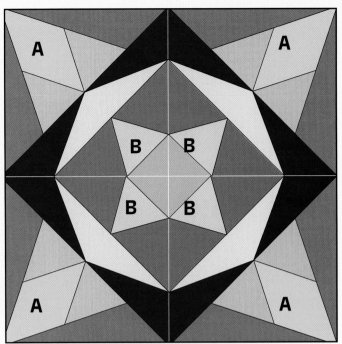

Unit Placement Diagram

DIAMONDS AND STARS
8" block (moderate)

1. Make four each of units A and B.

2. Sew each unit A to a unit B, matching at dots for assembly.

3. Sew four units A–B together, matching at dots for assembly.

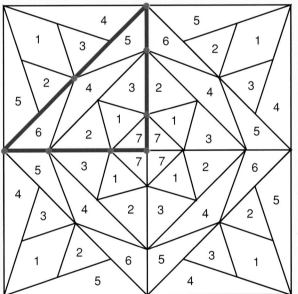

Seam Line Diagram

Diamonds and Stars Unit Pattern

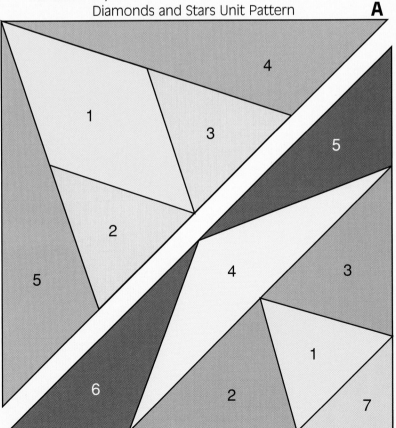

Diamonds and Stars Unit Pattern

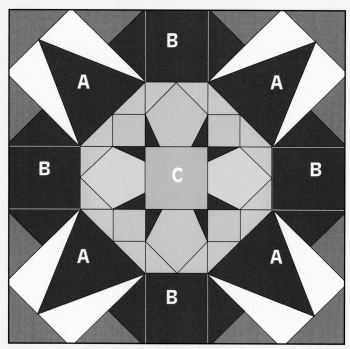

Unit Placement Diagram

STARRED DELIGHT
8" block (moderate)

Note: Pieces 7 and 7a, and 8 and 8a are preseamed before sewing to each unit A. See preseam instructions on page 8.

1. Make four each of units A and B.

2. Cut one 1½" square for unit C.

3. Sew a unit A to each side of a unit B, matching at dots for assembly. Repeat.

4. Sew remaining units B to each side of unit C.

5. Sew a unit A–B–A to top and bottom of assembled unit B–C–B, matching at dots for assembly.

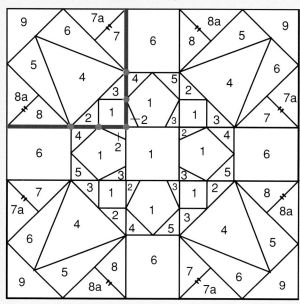

Seam Line Diagram

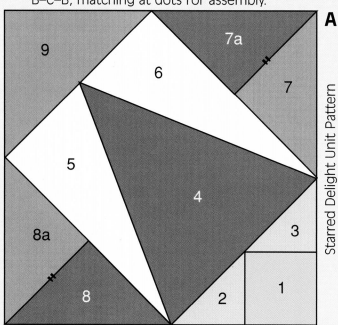

Starred Delight Unit Pattern

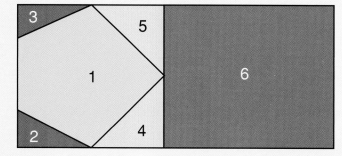

Starred Delight Unit Pattern

DWARF DAHLIA
4" block (moderate)

Note: Pieces 6 and 6a, and 7 and 7a are preseamed before sewing to each unit C. See preseam instructions on page 8.

1. Make one unit A. Make two each of units B and C.

2. Sew a unit B to each side of unit A, matching at dots for assembly.

3. Sew a unit C to top and bottom of unit B–A–B, matching at dots for assembly.

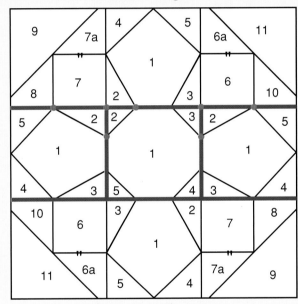

Unit Placement Diagram

Seam Line Diagram

Dwarf Dahlia
Unit Pattern

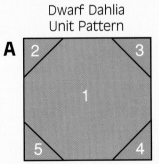

Dwarf Dahlia
Unit Pattern

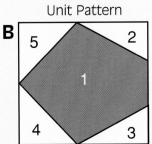

C Dwarf Dahlia Unit Pattern

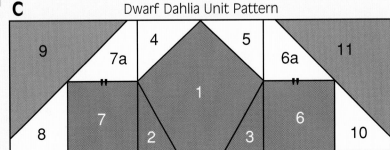

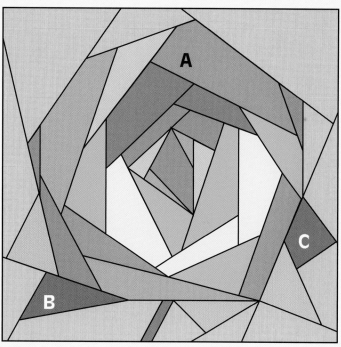

Unit Placement Diagram

Cabbage Rose

4" block (moderate)

Note: Pieces 31 and 31a are preseamed before sewing to unit A. See preseam instructions on page 8.

1. Make one each of units A, B, and C.

2. Clip unit B to seam line at dot. Sew units together in alphabetical order, matching at dot for assembly.

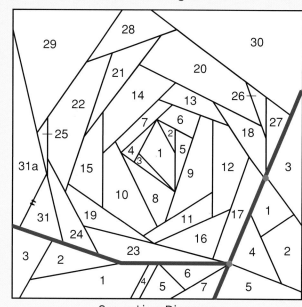

Seam Line Diagram

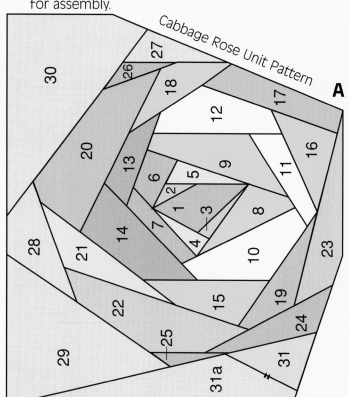

Cabbage Rose Unit Pattern

A

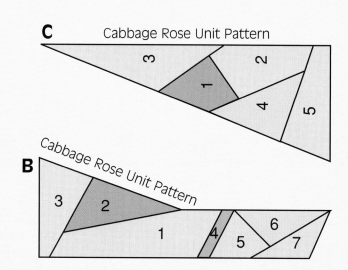

C   Cabbage Rose Unit Pattern

B   Cabbage Rose Unit Pattern

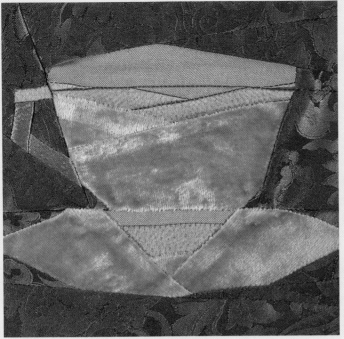

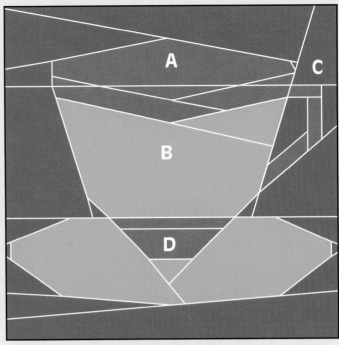

Unit Placement Diagram

TEA CUP
4" block (moderate)

1. Make one each of units A, B, C, and D.

2. Sew units together in alphabetical order, matching at dots for assembly.

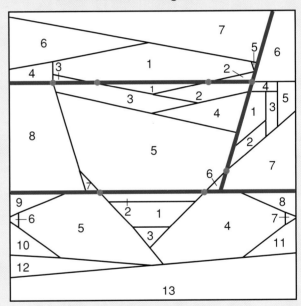

Seam Line Diagram

B
Tea Cup Unit Pattern

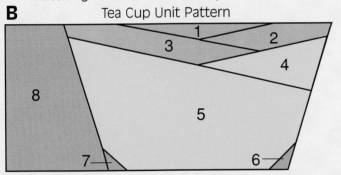

A
Tea Cup Unit Pattern

D
Tea Cup Unit Pattern

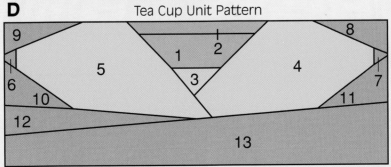

C
Tea Cup Unit Pattern

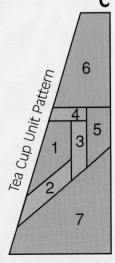

Victorian House
4" x 6" block (difficult)

1. Make one each of units A, B, C, D, and E. Make one mirror image of unit B.

2. Sew unit B to side of unit A. Repeat for mirror image unit B(m).

3. Clip unit D to seam line at center dot. Sew remaining units to unit B–A–B(m) in alphabetical order, matching at dots for assembly.

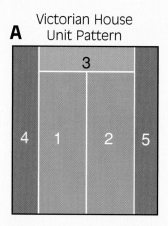

Victorian House
Unit Pattern

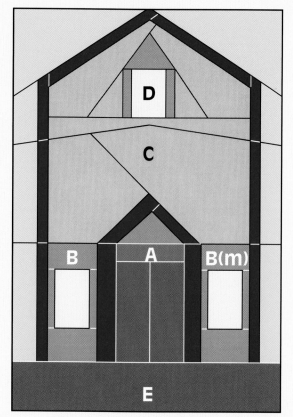

Unit Placement Diagram

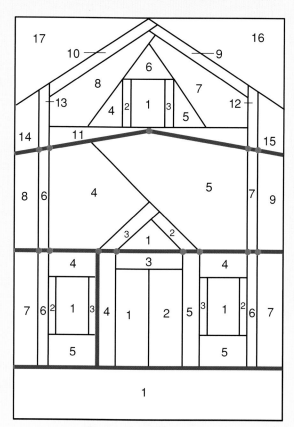

Seam Line Diagram

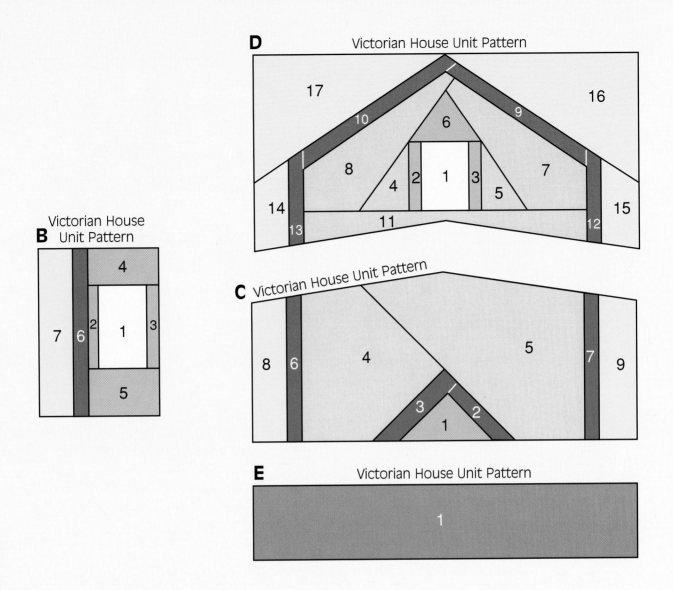

D Victorian House Unit Pattern

B Victorian House Unit Pattern

C Victorian House Unit Pattern

E Victorian House Unit Pattern

Note: See Dawn Flower block on page 102.

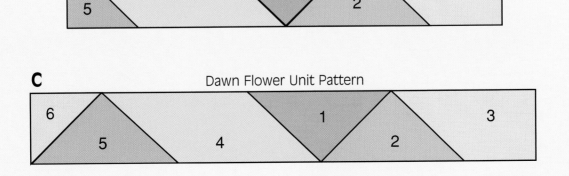

D Dawn Flower Unit Pattern

C Dawn Flower Unit Pattern

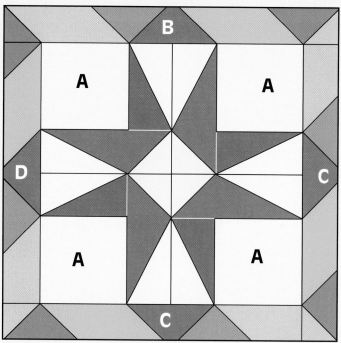

Unit Placement Diagram

Dawn Flower
6" block (difficult)

1. Make four each of unit A, alternating colors as shown. Make one each of units B and D. Make two of unit C, alternating colors as shown.

2. Sew four units A together, matching at dots for assembly.

3. Beginning with unit B and following in alphabetical order sew units B, D and D to outer edges of assembled unit A, matching dots for assembly.

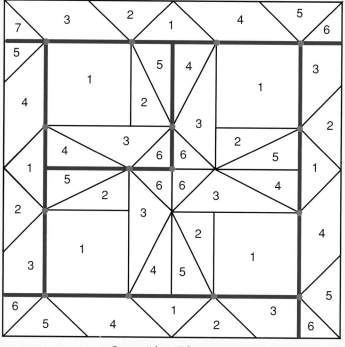

Seam Line Diagram

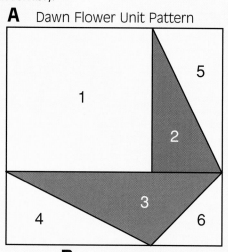

A Dawn Flower Unit Pattern

B Dawn Flower Unit Pattern

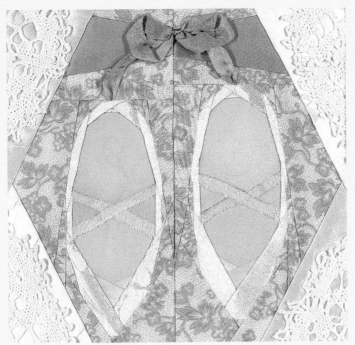

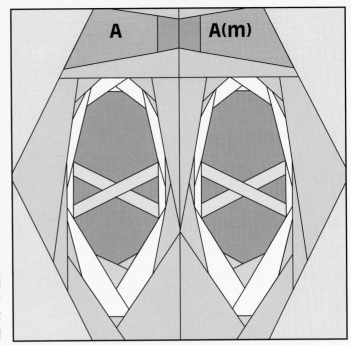

BALLET SHOES

Unit Placement Diagram

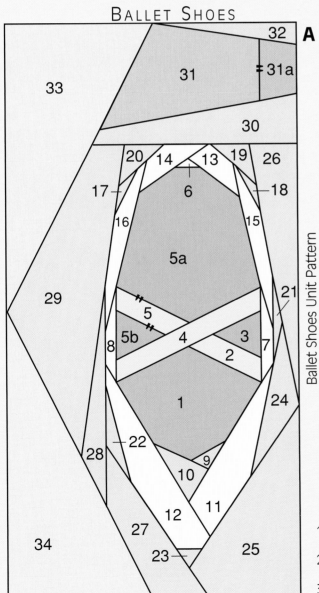

A

33

32
31   31a
30

20 14 13 19 26
17   18
6
16   15

5a

29

5
5b 4 3
8   2 7

1

21

24

28 22
10 9

27 12 11

34 23 25

Ballet Shoes Unit Pattern

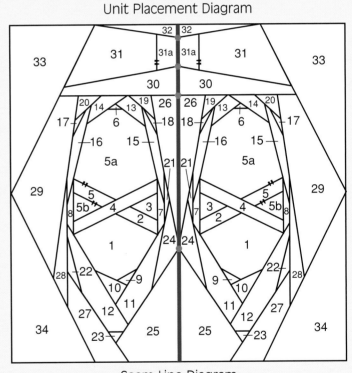

Seam Line Diagram

BALLET SHOES

6" block (difficult)

Note: Pieces 5, 5a, and 5b, and 31 and 31a are preseamed before sewing to unit A and mirror image unit A(m). See preseam instructions on page 8.

1. Make one unit A. Make one mirror image of unit A.

2. Sew unit A to unit A(m), matching at dots for assembly.

3. Embellish with ribbons to make ties and lace in corners.

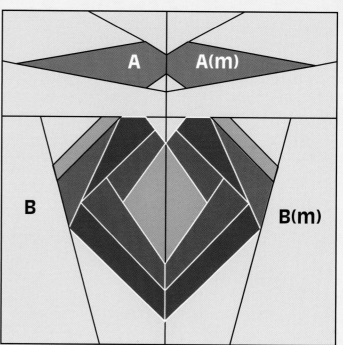

Unit Placement Diagram

HEART LOCKET
4" block (moderate)

1. Make one each of units A and B. Make one mirror image each of units A and B.

2. Sew each unit to its mirror image, matching at dots for assembly.

3. Sew unit A–A(m) to unit B–B(m), matching at dots for assembly.

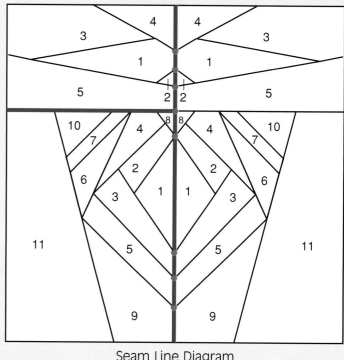

Seam Line Diagram

B Heart Locket Unit Pattern

A Heart Locket Unit Pattern

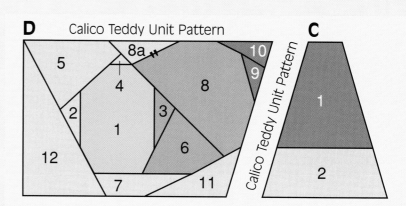

CALICO TEDDY
6" block (moderate)

Note: Pieces 8 and 8a, and 11 and 11a are preseamed before sewing to unit A and mirror image unit A(m). Pieces 8 and 8a are preseamed before sewing to unit D and mirror image unit D(m). See preseam instructions on page 8.

1. Make one each of units A, B, C, and D. Make one mirror image each of units A, B, and D.

2. Sew unit A to its mirror image, matching at dots for assembly. Repeat for unit B. End unit B seam at top center dot.

3. Sew unit A–A(m) to unit B–B(m), matching at dots for assembly.

4. Sew unit D to side of unit C, matching at dot for assembly. Repeat for mirror image unit D(m).

5. Sew unit A–A(m)–B–B(m) to unit D–C–D(m), matching at dots for assembly.

6. Sew ½" border to block.

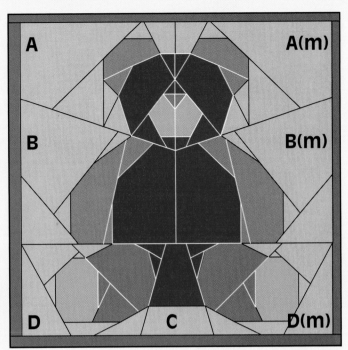

Unit Placement Diagram

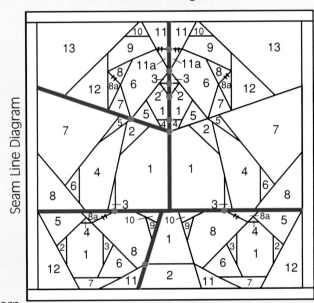

Seam Line Diagram

A Calico Teddy Unit Pattern

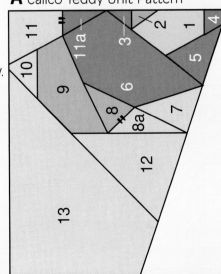

B Calico Teddy Unit Pattern

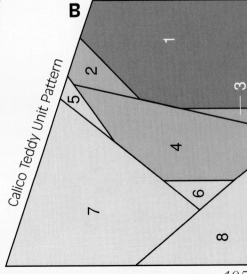

Chapter 11

Calico Country

Just one example of many quilt possibilities.

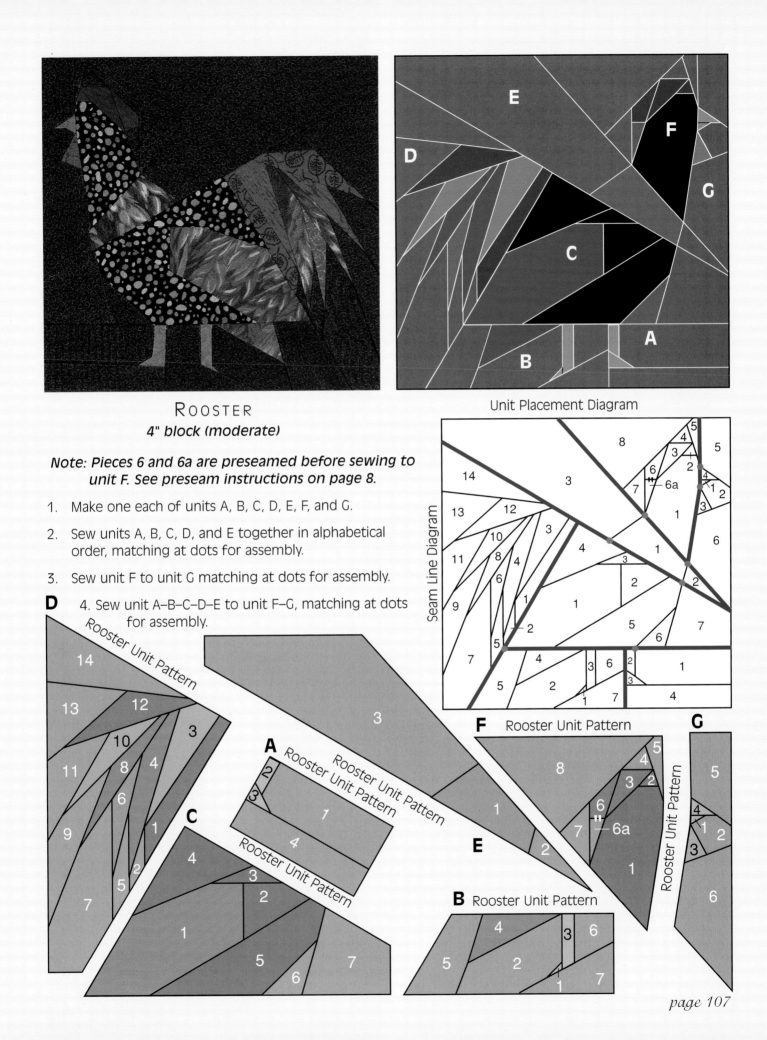

ROOSTER
4" block (moderate)

Note: Pieces 6 and 6a are preseamed before sewing to unit F. See preseam instructions on page 8.

1. Make one each of units A, B, C, D, E, F, and G.

2. Sew units A, B, C, D, and E together in alphabetical order, matching at dots for assembly.

3. Sew unit F to unit G matching at dots for assembly.

4. Sew unit A–B–C–D–E to unit F–G, matching at dots for assembly.

Unit Placement Diagram

Seam Line Diagram

D Rooster Unit Pattern

A Rooster Unit Pattern

Rooster Unit Pattern

C Rooster Unit Pattern

F Rooster Unit Pattern

G Rooster Unit Pattern

E

B Rooster Unit Pattern

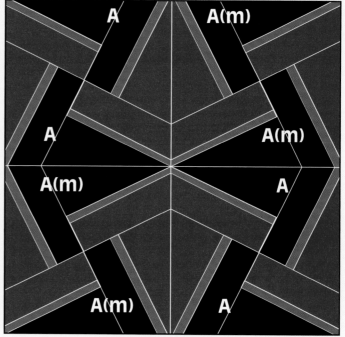

ARABIC LATTICE
8" block (difficult)

1. Make four of unit A. Make four mirror images of unit A.

2. Sew two units A together, forming a square. Repeat.

3. Sew two mirror image units A(m) together, forming a square. Repeat.

4. Sew each unit A–A to a unit A(m)–A(m), matching at dots for assembly.

5. Sew units A–A–A(m)–A(m) together, matching at dots for assembly.

Unit Placement Diagram

Seam Line Diagram

A

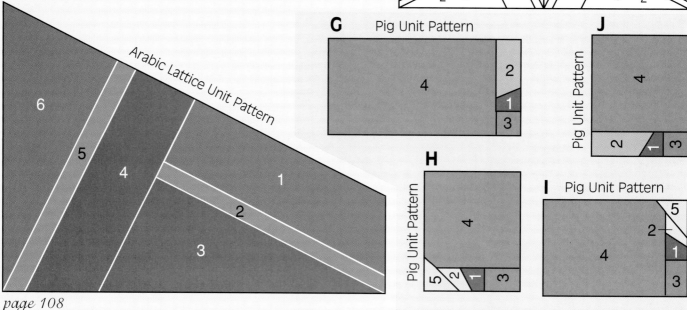

Arabic Lattice Unit Pattern

G Pig Unit Pattern

H Pig Unit Pattern

I Pig Unit Pattern

J Pig Unit Pattern

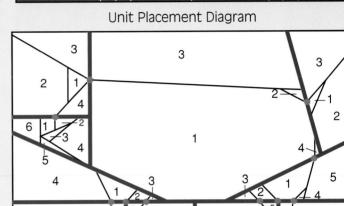

Unit Placement Diagram

Pɪɢ
4" x 6" block (moderate)

1. Make one each of units A, B, C, D, E, F, G, H, I, and J.

2. Sew unit A to unit B.

3. Sew unit C to unit D.

4. Sew unit A–B to unit C–D.

5. Sew unit E and unit F to unit A–B–C–D.

6. Sew units G, H, I, and J together in alphabetical order.

7. Sew unit A–B–C–D–E–F to unit G–H–I–J.

Seam Line Diagram

Pig Unit Pattern

F

C

Pig Unit Pattern

D Pig Unit Pattern

E

B Pig Unit Pattern

Pig Unit Pattern

A Pig Unit Pattern

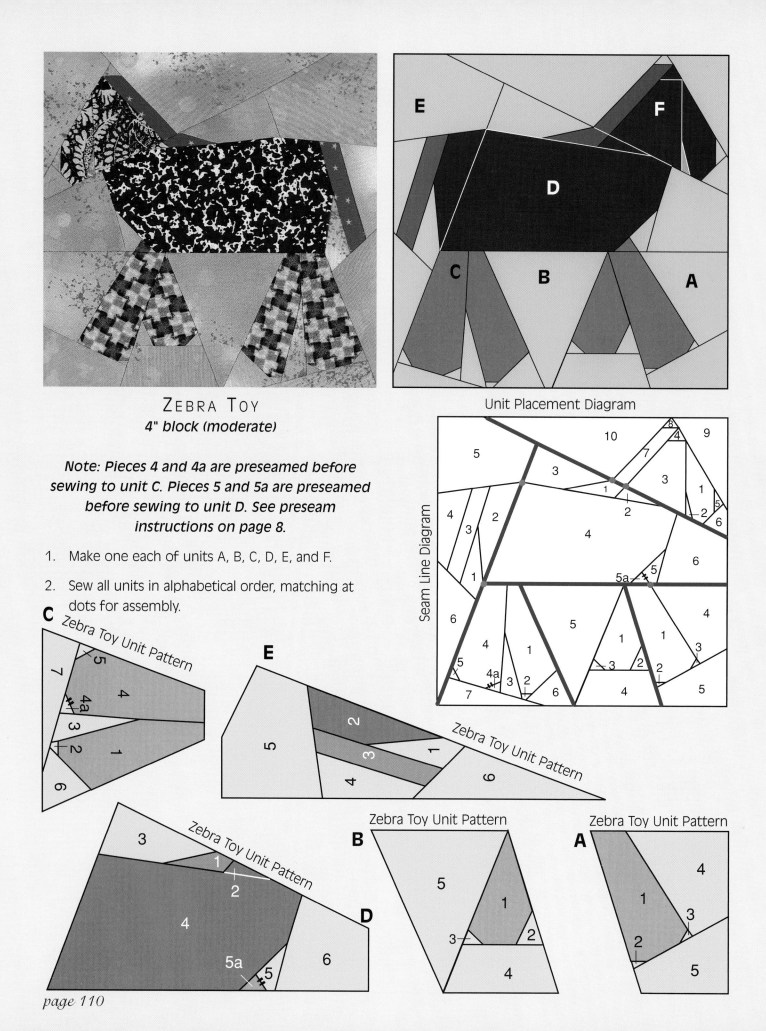

ZEBRA TOY
4" block (moderate)

Note: Pieces 4 and 4a are preseamed before sewing to unit C. Pieces 5 and 5a are preseamed before sewing to unit D. See preseam instructions on page 8.

1. Make one each of units A, B, C, D, E, and F.

2. Sew all units in alphabetical order, matching at dots for assembly.

Unit Placement Diagram

Seam Line Diagram

C Zebra Toy Unit Pattern

E Zebra Toy Unit Pattern

Zebra Toy Unit Pattern — D

B Zebra Toy Unit Pattern

A Zebra Toy Unit Pattern

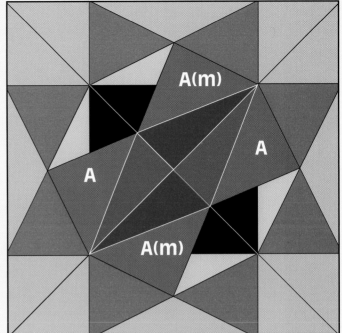

Unit Placement Diagram

CALICO STAR
6" block (moderate)

Note: Pieces 6 and 6a are preseamed before sewing to each unit. See preseam instructions on page 8.

1. Make two of unit A. Make two mirror images of unit A.

2. Sew each unit A to a mirror image, matching at dots for assembly.

3. Sew units A–A(m) together, matching at dots for assembly.

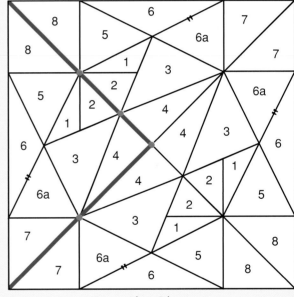

Seam Line Diagram

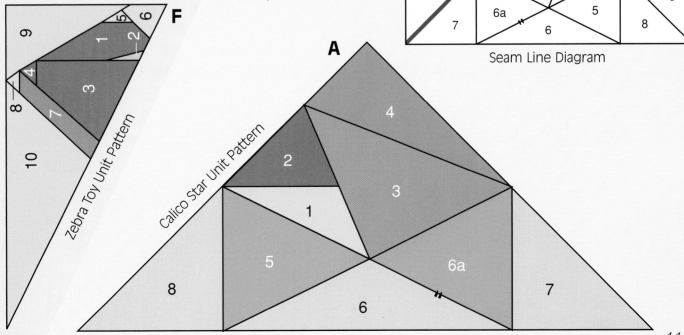

Chapter 12
Tropical Delight

Just one example of many quilt possibilities.

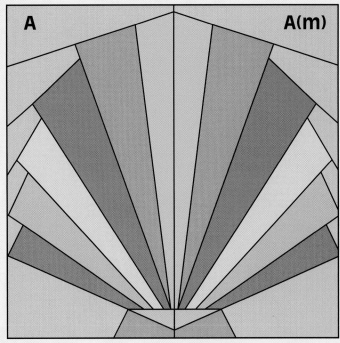

SCALLOP
4" block (moderate)

Unit Placement Diagram

Note: Pieces 13 and 13a are preseamed before sewing to unit A and mirror image of unit A. See preseam instructions on page 8.

1. Make one unit A. Make one mirror image of unit A.

2. Sew unit A to mirror image unit A(m), matching at dots for assembly.

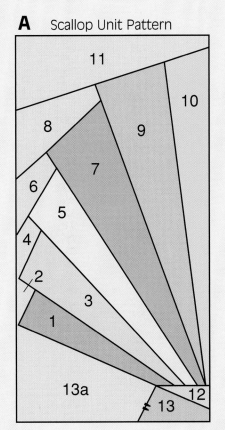

A Scallop Unit Pattern

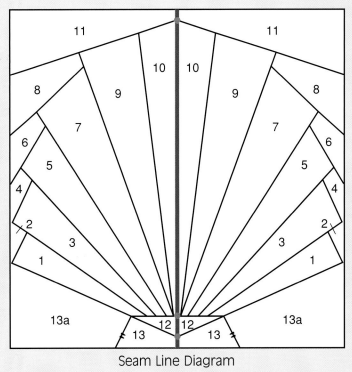

Seam Line Diagram

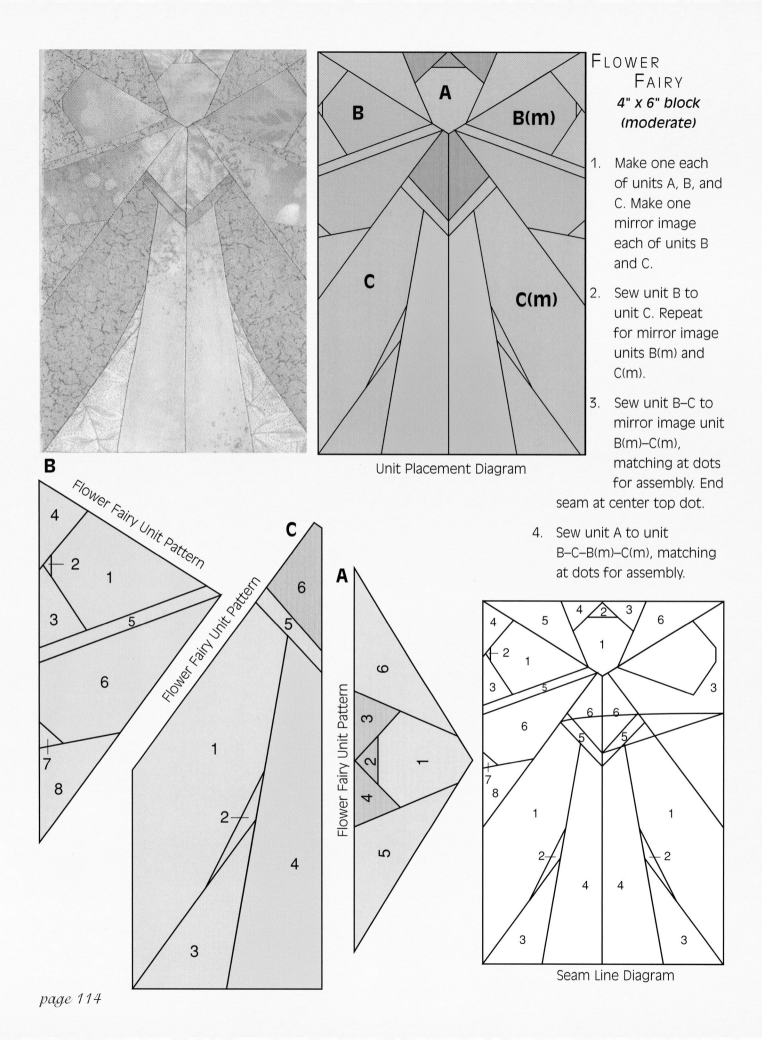

FLOWER FAIRY

4" x 6" block (moderate)

1. Make one each of units A, B, and C. Make one mirror image each of units B and C.

2. Sew unit B to unit C. Repeat for mirror image units B(m) and C(m).

3. Sew unit B–C to mirror image unit B(m)–C(m), matching at dots for assembly. End seam at center top dot.

4. Sew unit A to unit B–C–B(m)–C(m), matching at dots for assembly.

Unit Placement Diagram

B

Flower Fairy Unit Pattern

C

Flower Fairy Unit Pattern

A

Flower Fairy Unit Pattern

Seam Line Diagram

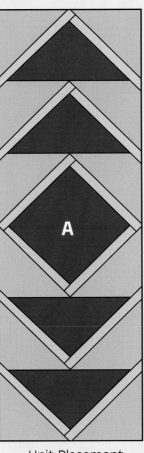

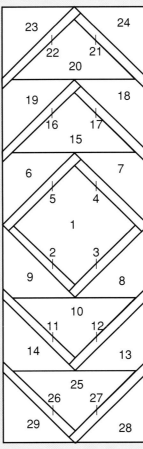

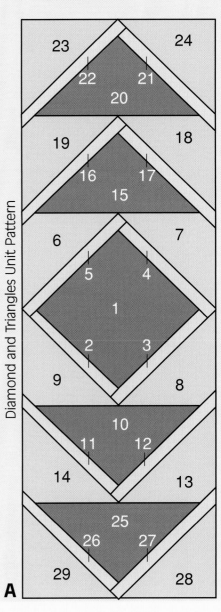

Diamond and Triangles
2" x 6" block (easy)

1. Make one unit A.

Unit Placement Diagram

Seam Line Diagram

Diamond and Triangles Unit Pattern

A

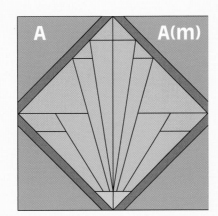

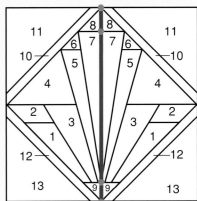

Lotus Blossom
2" block (moderate)

1. Make one unit A. Make one mirror image of unit A.

2. Sew unit A to mirror image unit A(m), matching at dots for assembly.

Unit Placement Diagram

Seam Line Diagram

A Lotus Blossom Unit Pattern

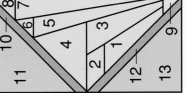

SUMMER ROSE

Unit Placement Diagram

A

Summer Rose Unit Pattern

B

Summer Rose Unit Pattern

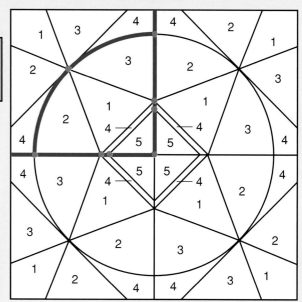

Seam Line Diagram

SUMMER ROSE
8" block (moderate)

1. Make four each of units A and B.

2. Cut close to seam line along curved edge of each unit A.

3. Sew each unit A to a unit B, matching at dots for assembly.

4. Sew four units A–B together, matching at dots for assembly.

SUNBURST
6" block (moderate)

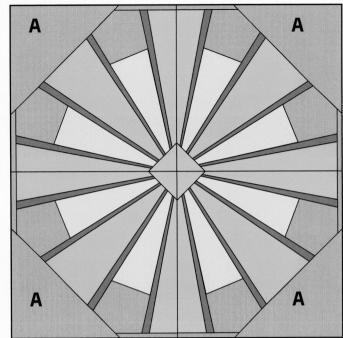

Unit Placement Diagram

Note: Pieces 6 and 6a are preseamed before sewing to each unit. See preseam instructions on page 8.

1. Make four each of unit A.

2. Sew four units A together, matching at dots for assembly.

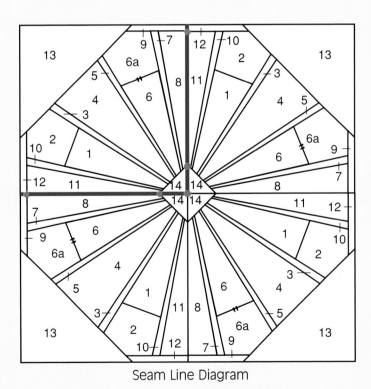

Seam Line Diagram

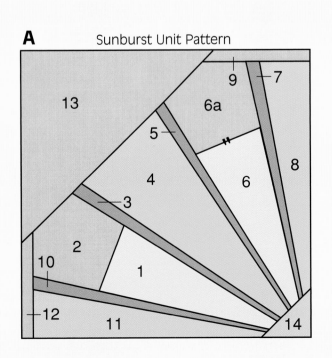

A Sunburst Unit Pattern

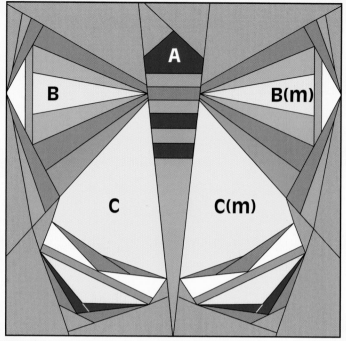

BUTTERFLY

Unit Placement Diagram

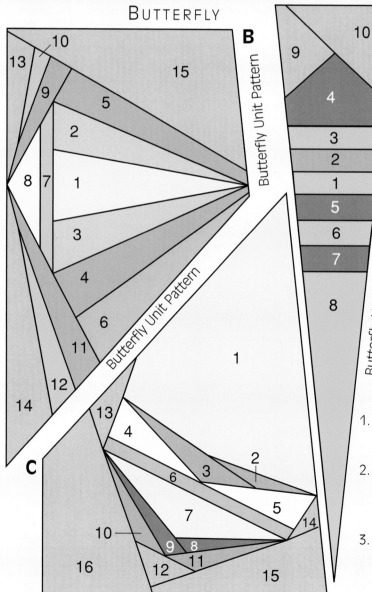

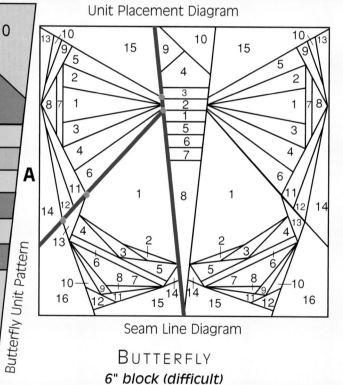

Seam Line Diagram

BUTTERFLY
6" block (difficult)

1. Make one each of units A, B, and C. Make one mirror image each of units B and C.

2. Sew unit B to unit C, matching at dots for assembly. Repeat for mirror image units B(m) and C(m).

3. Sew unit B–C to a side of unit A, matching at dots for assembly. Repeat for mirror image unit B(m)–C(m).

S U N R I S E

4" block (easy)

Unit Placement Diagram

1. Make one unit A.

Sunrise Unit Pattern

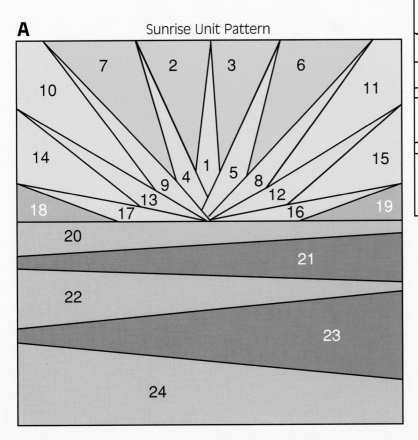

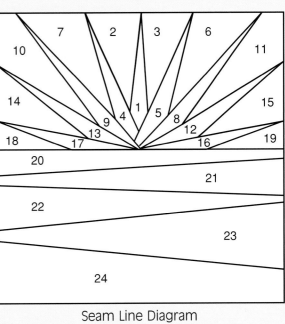

Seam Line Diagram

Chapter 13

Traditional

Just one example of many quilt possibilities.

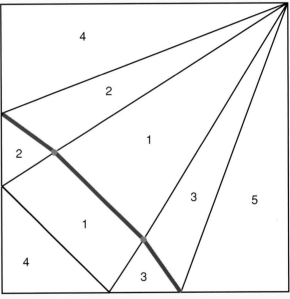

Unit Placement Diagram

ARROWHEAD
4" block (easy)

Note: This block may be made as an 8" block by joining four blocks.

1. Make one each of units A and B.

2. Clip unit B to seam line at inside dots.

3. Sew unit A to unit B, matching at dots for assembly.

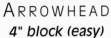

Seam Line Diagram

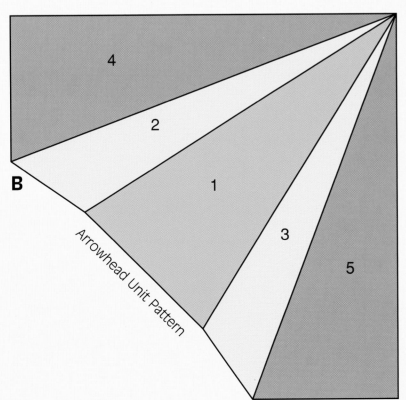

B

Arrowhead Unit Pattern

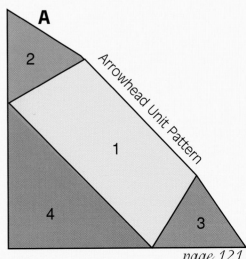

A

Arrowhead Unit Pattern

EARTH STAR
8" block (moderate)

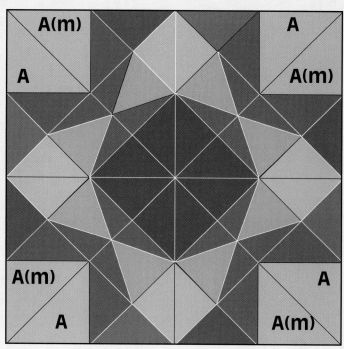

Unit Placement Diagram

Note: Pieces 7 and 7a are preseamed before sewing to each unit. See preseam instructions on page 8.

1. Make four of unit A. Make four mirror images of unit A.

2. Sew each unit A to a mirror image unit A(m), matching at dots for assembly.

3. Sew four units A–A(m) together, matching at dots for assembly.

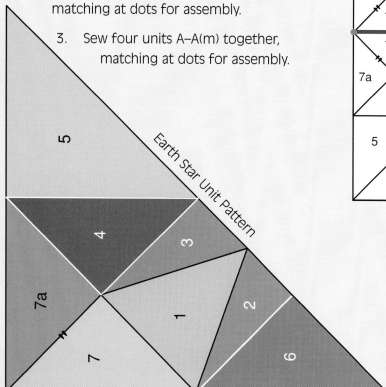

Earth Star Unit Pattern

Seam Line Diagram

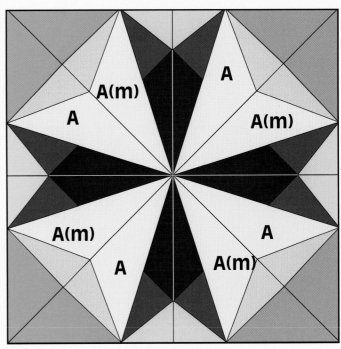

Unit Placement Diagram

FORTUNE'S FANCY
8" block (moderate)

Note: Pieces 4 and 4a are preseamed before sewing to each unit A and each mirror image unit A(m). See preseam instructions on page 8.

1. Make four of unit A. Make four mirror images of unit A.

2. Sew each unit A to a mirror image unit A(m), matching at dots for assembly.

3. Sew four units A–A(m) together, matching at dots for assembly.

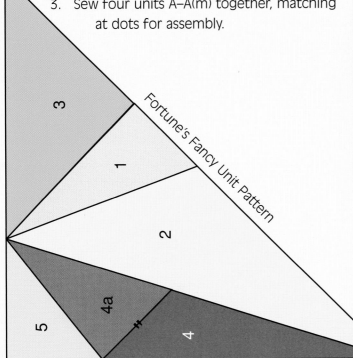

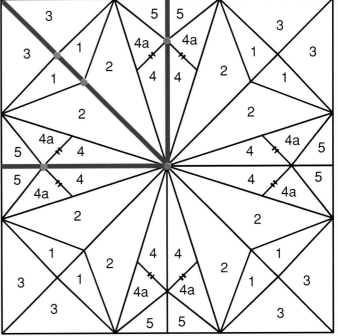

Seam Line Diagram

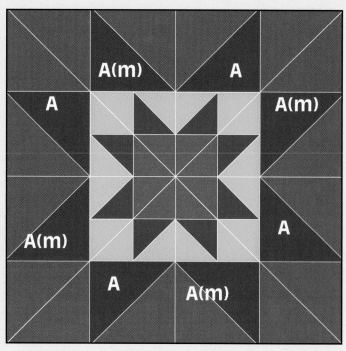

STARS AND SQUARES
8" block (moderate)

Unit Placement Diagram

1. Make four of unit A. Make four mirror images of unit A.

2. Sew each unit A to a mirror image unit A(m), matching at dots for assembly.

3. Sew four units A–A(m) together, matching at dots for assembly.

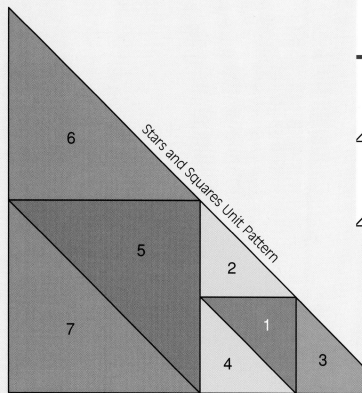

Seam Line Diagram

Stars and Squares Unit Pattern

A

LEAF
2" block (easy)

Note: This block may be made as a 4" block by joining four blocks.

1. Make one unit A.

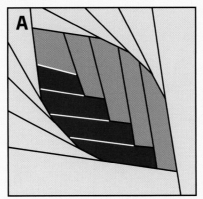

Unit Placement Diagram

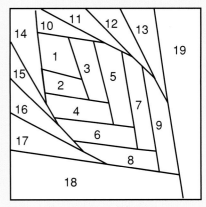

Seam Line Diagram

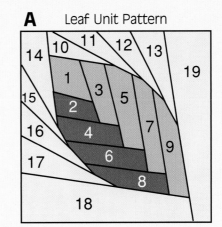

A Leaf Unit Pattern

FAN
2" block (easy)

1. Make one unit A.

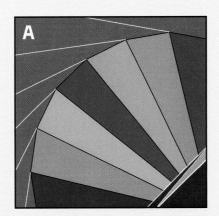

Unit Placement Diagram

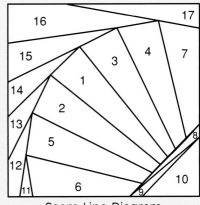

Seam Line Diagram

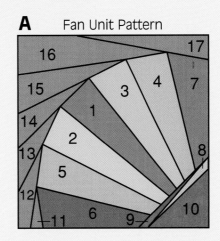

A Fan Unit Pattern

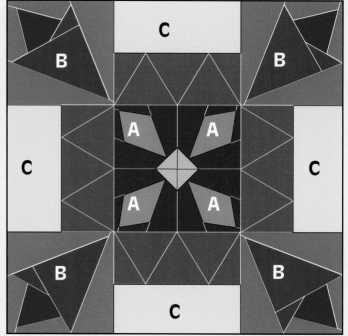

Unit Placement Diagram

CROSSROAD
8" block (moderate)

Note: Use striped oriental fabric to create pattern shown in unit C.

1. Make four each of units A, B, and C.

2. Sew a unit B to each side of a unit C, matching at dots for assembly. Repeat.

3. Sew four units A together for a 3" block, matching at dots for assembly.

4. Sew a unit C to each side of unit A, matching at dots for assembly.

5. Sew one unit B–C to top and one to bottom of unit A–C, matching at dots for assembly.

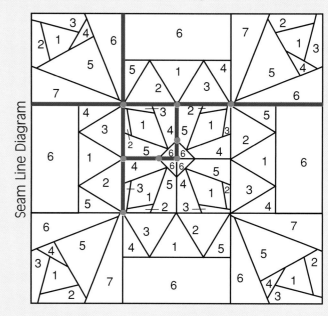

Seam Line Diagram

C   Crossroad Unit Pattern

B   Crossroad Unit Pattern

Crossroad Unit Pattern

A

Mary Jo Hiney learned sewing skills from her mother. These skills she refines to an art. Known for her intriguing fabric covered boxes and beautiful ribbon-work, Mary Jo now brings you original quilt block designs—made easy with the technique of foundation piecing.

Mary Jo attended the Los Angeles Fashion Institute of Design and Merchandising. She worked in the wardrobe department of NBC Studios in Burbank, California, where she dressed such stars as Lucille Ball and Maureen O'Hara.

dedicated to the fruit of love's spirit

to love's strength — joy

to love's security — peace

to love's endurance — patience

to love's conduct — kindness

to love's character — goodness

to love's confidence — faithfulness

to love's humility — gentleness

to love's victory — self-control

Metric Conversion Chart

cm—Centimetres
Inches to Centimetres

Inches	cm	Inches	cm	Inches	cm	Inches	cm
⅛	0.3	5	12.7	21	53.3	38	96.5
¼	0.6	6	15.2	22	55.9	39	99.1
½	1.3	7	17.8	23	58.4	40	101.6
⅝	1.6	8	20.3	24	61.0	41	104.1
¾	1.9	9	22.9	25	63.5	42	106.7
⅞	2.2	10	25.4	26	66.0	43	109.2
1	2.5	11	27.9	27	68.6	44	111.8
1¼	3.2	12	30.5	28	71.1	45	114.3
1½	3.8	13	33.0	29	73.7	46	116.8
1¾	4.4	14	35.6	30	76.2	47	119.4
2	5.1	15	38.1	31	78.7	48	121.9
2½	6.4	16	40.6	33	83.8	49	124.5
3	7.6	17	43.2	34	86.4	50	127.0
3½	8.9	18	45.7	35	88.9		
4	10.2	19	48.3	36	91.4		
4½	11.4	20	50.8	37	94.0		

Index